IEPs: Writing Quality Individualized Education Programs

THIRD EDITION

IEPs: Writing Quality Individualized Education Programs

THIRD EDITION

Gordon S. Gibb
Brigham Young University

Tina Taylor Dyches
Brigham Young University

PEARSON

Boston   Columbus   Indianapolis   New York   San Francisco   Hoboken
Amsterdam   Cape Town   Dubai   London   Madrid   Milan   Munich   Paris   Montreal   Toronto
Delhi   Mexico City   São Paulo   Sydney   Hong Kong   Seoul   Singapore   Taipei   Tokyo

Vice President and Editorial Director: Jeffery W.
    Johnston
Executive Editor: Ann Castel Davis
Editorial Assistant: Janelle Criner
Executive Field Marketing Manager: Krista Clark
Senior Product Marketing Manager: Christopher
    Barry
Senior Project Manager: Marilyn Lloyd
Program Manager: Joe Sweeney
Operations Specialist: Deidra Skahill
Text Designer: Aptara

Cover Design Director: Diane Ernsberger
Cover Image: Superstock
Media Producer: Autumn Benson
Media Project Manager: Tammy Walters
Full-Service Project Management: Jogender
    Taneja/Aptara
Composition: Aptara
Printer/Binder: LSC Communications
Cover Printer: LSC Communications
Text Font: CharterITCbyBT-Roman

Library of Congress Cataloging-in-Publication Data is available from the Publisher upon request

PEARSON

ISBN-10: 0-13-394952-4
ISBN-13: 978-0-13-394952-0

Table of Contents

Preface

Welcome to *IEPs: Writing Quality Individualized Education Programs,* 3rd Edition

We designed this guide for anyone involved in the special education of students with disabilities. It is useful for parents, preservice and inservice education professionals, and others who support families or provide services to these students. We know that many of you regularly serve, or will serve, on teams that provide educational services to students with disabilities, and you will likely be responsible for contributing to the development of individualized education programs (IEPs). This guide will facilitate your collaborative work on these teams.

Our goal is to help you write quality IEPs. Since the IEP is a legal document that guides the education of students with disabilities, it is critical that you gain the skills and knowledge to create IEPs that meet the standards of the law. To help you gain a deeper understanding of this process, we have organized this guide with several helpful features:

- Summary of the Individuals with Disabilities Education Improvement Act (IDEA) 2004 in language that is easy to understand

- Organization of the IEP process into seven manageable steps

- Explanation, modeling, practice, and feedback for each step

- Brief procedural summary at the end of each step

We have also added several new features:

- Emphasis on standards-based IEPs aligned with core curricula

- Writing standards-based goals for students achieving well below grade level

- Role of response to intervention (RTI)

- New sample IEPs for four students with varying disabilities and ages, including transition planning

- Alignment with the requirements of the No Child Left Behind (NCLB) Act

- A personal guide, Ms. Mentor, to provide comments, directions, and suggestions as you read and complete each step in the guide

Assumptions Behind This Guide

In developing this guide, we have assumed that you and the rest of the school team have completed the identification, referral, evaluation, and classification processes for your students with disabilities. This guide begins at the point when your team is ready to develop students' IEPs.

Parameters for This Guide

This guide does not address planning for students without disabilities who struggle in school. Students whose primary language is not English or whose learning difficulties are caused by environmental, cultural, or economic disadvantages, or those students who have not received appropriate instruction are not eligible for special education and therefore do not need an IEP unless they also have a disability. These students may be served by other programs such as bilingual education, Title 1, or Section 504 of the Rehabilitation Act.

Legal Basis for This Guide

Federal law mandates the special education process, so we have structured this guide in accordance with federal law and regulations, and we use terminology from the federal law throughout the text. Individual states must meet the requirements of the federal law, but each state may also add specific state policies and procedures. You should consult your state and district regulations for their specific policies, procedures, and terminology.

Acknowledgments

We express our gratitude to Sharon Black for her excellent editing and proofreading and to Ann Davis at Pearson for her patient support of our efforts in completing this third edition.

We would also like to thank the reviewers of this edition:
Michael E. May, Southern Illinois University; Theodore Pikes, North Carolina Central University; and Barbara J. Wiese, St. Ambrose University.

—GSG and TTD

About the Authors

Gordon S. Gibb, PhD, *taught students with disabilities in the public schools for 16 years prior to his appointment at Brigham Young University. As associate professor and Director of Undergraduate Special Education Dr. Gibb prepares teachers to work with students with mild to moderate disabilities and conducts instructional improvement activities in several schools. His research centers on cultural models for understanding disability and on effective instruction for students with disabilities. Dr. Gibb enjoys cycling, cooking, studying, family, and the outdoors.*

Tina Taylor Dyches, EdD, *is a professor and associate dean in the McKay School of Education at Brigham Young University. Dr. Dyches has worked with individuals with significant disabilities and their families for nearly 30 years as a special educator and professor. Her service and research interests include adaptation of families raising children with disabilities, children's literature that characterizes individuals with disabilities, and provision of appropriate services to individuals with disabilities. Dr. Dyches enjoys spending time with family, playing sports, traveling, and reading.*

Introduction: Special Education and the Individualized Education Program

Before Mom found an opportunity to go down to the grade school office to register me, three members of the school board came to visit us. . . . "It has been brought to my attention that you folks have a son in a wheelchair. It is our duty to inform you he will be unable to attend school" (Warren & Kirkendall, 1973, p. 91).

Don Kirkendall was a young boy partially paralyzed by polio in the early 20th century. His experience typifies the lack of public school opportunities for American children and youth with disabilities until later in that century. Prior to 1975, there was no universally applicable law that required states or schools to help these children learn. In 1970, only one in five children with disabilities received schooling, and some states specifically excluded children with certain disabilities from attending public schools (Office of Special Education Programs, 2000). Reasons for exclusion included inconvenience to school personnel, lack of teacher expertise, and fears of other children being adversely affected by associating with children with disabilities. Many individuals with disabilities were housed in institutions, often with minimal care and insufficient food, clothing, and shelter (Office of Special Education Programs, 2000). Fortunately, the tide of civil rights legislation in the 1950s and 1960s, along with increased public advocacy and a series of pivotal legal decisions, moved Congress to pass the Education for all Handicapped Children Act in 1975, mandating free and appropriate public education for all children, regardless of disability. The 2004 Individuals with Disabilities Education Improvement Act (IDEA), the current version of this landmark law, governs special education in the United States.

What is special education?

In this section, we present several questions that parents, preservice teachers, related service providers, teachers, and others ask about IDEA and special education in general. We answer these questions to provide a foundation for the remainder of the book. For more information about IDEA, see http://idea.ed.gov.

IDEA defines special education as follows:

Specially designed instruction, at no cost to parents, to meet the unique needs of a student with a disability, including instruction conducted in the classroom, in the home, in hospitals and institutions, and in other settings; and instruction in physical education. (34 CFR §300.39)

Special education is not a place, like a resource room or self-contained classroom, but is "specially designed instruction" provided in whatever setting the individualized education program (IEP) team determines is appropriate. To provide special education, each state must ensure that all students ages 3 to 21 with disabilities who reside in the state have access to these five provisions: (1) free appropriate public education, (2) appropriate evaluation,

(3) individualized education program, (4) least restrictive environment, and (5) procedural safeguards. The following statements are quoted from the referenced sections of the law; they are organized with bullet points and bold has been added for clarity and emphasis.

1. **Free Appropriate Public Education.** This is defined as special education and related services that

   - are provided to students with disabilities at public expense, under public supervision, and without charge,
   - meet the standards of the state educational agency,
   - include appropriate preschool, elementary school, or secondary school education, and
   - are provided consistent with each student's individualized education program. (34 CFR §300.17)

2. **Appropriate Evaluation.** To serve a student in special education, a school must first conduct an evaluation to determine if the student has a disability, if the disability inhibits progress in the general curriculum, and if special education is needed to meet the student's individual needs. This evaluation must use a variety of assessment tools and strategies to gather relevant functional, developmental, and academic information to determine if a student has a disability and to assist in determining the content of the IEP. The evaluation should include information about the student provided by the parent. In order for the evaluation to be appropriate it should

   - avoid relying on any single measure or assessment to determine if a student has a disability,
   - use technically sound instruments that may assess the relative contribution of cognitive and behavioral factors, in addition to physical or developmental factors,
   - be selected and administered with care to avoid racial or cultural discrimination,
   - be provided and administered in the language and communication form most likely to yield accurate information on what the student knows and can do academically, developmentally, and functionally, unless this is not feasible,
   - use instruments that are valid and reliable, administered by trained and knowledgeable personnel,
   - assess the student in all areas of suspected disability, and
   - allow for coordination between schools for students who transfer from one agency to another in the same academic year. (34 CFR §300.304)

3. **Individualized Education Program.** If the results of the evaluation indicate that a student needs special education, then an individualized education program (IEP) must be developed. The IEP, developed by a team, is a document that includes the following, with the key steps in bold print.

   - A statement of the student's **present levels of academic achievement and functional performance**, including
     a. how the disability affects the student's involvement and progress in the general education curriculum, or
     b. for preschool students, how the disability affects participation in appropriate activities,

- A statement of **measurable annual goals**, including academic and functional goals, designed
  a. to meet the student's needs that result from the disability, enabling the student to be involved in and make progress in the general curriculum, and
  b. to meet each of the student's other educational needs that result from the disability, and
  c. for students who take alternate assessments aligned with alternate achievement standards, a description of benchmarks, or short-term objectives.
- A description of how the **student's progress** toward meeting the annual goals will be measured and when periodic reports on the student's progress will be provided.
- A statement of the **special education, related services, and supplementary aids and services**, based on peer-reviewed research to the extent practicable, to be provided to the student
  a. to advance toward attaining the annual goals,
  b. to be involved in and make progress in the general education curriculum, and
  c. to participate in extracurricular and other nonacademic activities.
- An explanation of the extent, if any, to which the student **will not participate** with nondisabled students in the regular class and in extracurricular and other nonacademic activities.
- A statement of any individual appropriate **accommodations** that are necessary to measure the academic achievement and functional performance of the student on state and districtwide assessments, and if the IEP team determines that the student shall take an alternate assessment, explanations of
  a. why the student cannot participate in the regular assessment, and
  b. which alternate assessment has been selected as appropriate for the student.
- The **projected date** for the beginning of the IEP and the anticipated frequency, location, and duration of the services and modifications.
- A **transition plan** beginning not later than the first IEP to be in effect when the student is 16, and updated annually thereafter, including
  a. appropriate measurable postsecondary goals based upon age-appropriate transition assessments related to training, education, employment, and, where appropriate, independent living skills,
  b. the transition services, including courses of study, needed to assist the student in reaching those goals, and
  c. beginning not later than one year before the student reaches the age of majority under state law, a statement that the student has been informed of the rights that will transfer to him or her on reaching the age of majority. (CFR §300.320)

4. **Least Restrictive Environment (LRE).** This means that students with disabilities will be educated with students without disabilities to the maximum extent appropriate. These learning environments include public or private institutions or other care facilities. Special classes, separate schooling, or other removal of students with disabilities from the regular educational environment occurs only when the nature or severity of a student's disability

is such that education in regular classes with the use of supplementary aids and services cannot be achieved satisfactorily. (34 CFR §300.114)

WHAT IS APPROPRIATE? EDUCATING STUDENTS WITH DISABILITIES WITH NONDISABLED PEERS TO THE "MAXIMUM EXTENT **APPROPRIATE**" IS DIFFERENT THAN DOING SO TO THE "MAXIMUM EXTENT POSSIBLE." THE LAW DOES NOT INSIST ON FULL INCLUSION IN THE GENERAL EDUCATION CLASSROOM IF THIS PLACEMENT DOES NOT MEET THE STUDENT'S NEEDS.

5. **Procedural Safeguards.** Schools must establish and maintain procedures to ensure that students with disabilities and their parents are guaranteed procedural safeguards as a free appropriate public education is provided. A document explaining these procedural safeguards or "parents' rights" must be given to parents annually, typically at or before the IEP meeting. The document must be in the native language of the parents, unless use of this language is clearly not feasible, and must be written in an easily understandable style. The document must include a full explanation of the following safeguards:

- Parents may present information from an independent educational evaluation to be considered in determining the existence of a disability and/or designating the contents of the IEP.

- Parents must be provided with written notice and provide written consent before any action is taken with regard to the education of their child with a disability.

- Parents have access to their child's educational records.

- Parents have the opportunity to present and participate in resolving complaints through mediation or due process.

- Parents should receive an explanation of the procedures for due process hearings.

- Parents have the right to keep their child in the current placement pending and during a due process hearing.

- Parents should receive an explanation of procedures for students who are subject to placement in an interim alternative educational setting.

- Parents should be provided an explanation of the requirements for unilateral placement parents may make of students in private schools at public expense.

- Parents should receive an explanation of state-level appeals.

- Parents should receive an explanation of procedures for civil actions.

- Parents should receive an explanation of attorney's fees. (34 CFR §300.500-536)

These five principles have been important aspects of special education since the first law was passed in 1975. The requirements for each principle have been altered somewhat in subsequent reauthorizations of IDEA, but the basic framework of special education in the United States has remained the same.

Now that you know the legal requirements for providing special education, you should understand how the process begins and what it involves. We discuss these topics next.

How does the special education process begin?

The special education process begins when a parent or a teacher makes a formal referral for evaluation to determine if a child has a disability. If the disability was evident before or soon after the child was born or during the preschool years, parents make the referral. But most disabilities are identified when a student does not achieve as expected in school and a teacher makes the referral.

RESPONSE TO INTERVENTION

Response to intervention (RTI), sometimes called multi-tiered system of support (MTSS), is a schoolwide approach to meeting students' needs based on how well they respond to various levels of instruction. Figure 1 depicts the graduated levels of support for academic and behavioral needs, focusing first on the general classroom and moving to more intensive support in smaller groups as needed. RTI is an excellent way to ensure that students receive appropriate research-based interventions that may meet their needs without referral for special education services.

When the classroom teacher's efforts to provide interventions for a struggling child are not successful at meeting the child's needs, the teacher should initiate a referral to determine if the student has a disability. The teacher must provide evidence that the child has participated in scientific, research-based interventions to address his or her individual needs, including data about the student's response to the interventions. If appropriate assessment indicates that the student has a disability and is eligible for special education services, then an IEP is developed.

What is the role of the IEP in special education?

The IEP is a legal document with two essential roles. First, it is the individualized component of special education planning, defining what *appropriate* means in the specific student's free appropriate public education. The IEP describes a student's special education program for one year, including goals for improvement and ways the school will help the student achieve the goals. The IEP emphasizes ways to help the student make progress in the general curriculum and participate with her or his peers without disabilities in extracurricular activities of an appropriate nature and extent. The IEP might be viewed as a personal road map for a student's education and school experience.

Figure 1. Response to intervention (RTI).

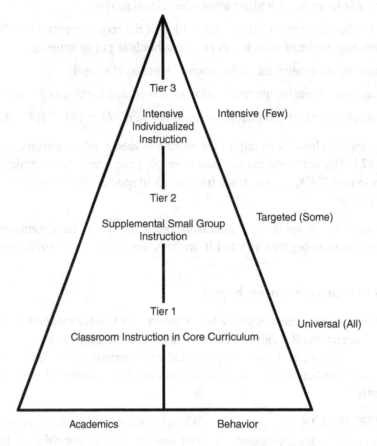

Tier 3

Intensive Individualized Instruction

Intensive (Few)

Tier 2

Supplemental Small Group Instruction

Targeted (Some)

Tier 1

Classroom Instruction in Core Curriculum

Universal (All)

Academics

Behavior

Second, the IEP serves as a basis for communication between parents and teachers regarding the student's educational growth and achievement. When both parents and teachers know the goals for the student's improvement, they have common reference points for discussion and decisions.

Who needs an IEP?

Any student between the ages of 3 and 21 who receives special education services must have a current IEP. To verify that a student is eligible for special education, three questions must be answered, with necessary evidence and explanation:

- Does the student have a disability?
- Does the disability inhibit progress in the general curriculum?
- Does the student require specially designed instruction to progress in the general curriculum?

Some students might have a disability that does not have a significant impact on their progress in the general curriculum. Such students might be eligible to receive classroom accommodations under Section 504 of the Rehabilitation Act of 1973 (29 U.S.C. §701). For example, a student with a mild visual impairment might require large-print materials in class, but she or he may not need specially designed instruction. With a 504 plan, the classroom teacher would provide large-print materials and other necessary adaptations or accommodations (e.g., front-row seating or additional time for tasks that require reading), but an IEP and special education services would not be required.

Are IEPs created for children with disabilities who are younger than 3 years or older than 21 years?

No. Special education is provided for infants and toddlers below the age of 3 who have been diagnosed with disabilities or developmental delays, but such interventions are based on an individualized family service plan (IFSP) instead of an IEP (U.S.C. 34 §636). The IFSP focuses not only on the needs of the child but also on the concerns, needs, and resources of the family. Developmentally appropriate services are provided in natural environments, such as the child's home, by members of an interdisciplinary team. The IFSP facilitates the child's transition to preschool or other services, or discontinues special education services that are no longer needed.

Adults with disabilities are not eligible for special education services after their 22nd birthday; therefore, these individuals do not have IEPs. From this age onward, individuals who still need services must depend on family or community support or on government agencies to meet their needs. Unfortunately, there is no guarantee that services will be available for all adults with disabilities who need them. Availability of services for adults with disabilities varies greatly across the United States.

Who develops the IEP?

The IEP is developed by a team that meets and discusses relevant information about the student's strengths and needs. IDEA states that the IEP team must consist of these members:

- The parents or guardians of the student with a disability
- At least one regular education teacher of the student if the student is or may be participating in the regular class
- At least one special education teacher or one special education provider
- A representative of the local education agency (LEA), usually the principal, who is qualified to provide or supervise the provision of special education for the student, is knowledgeable about the general education curriculum, and is knowledgeable about the availability of resources
- An individual who can interpret evaluation results (possibly one of those already mentioned on this list), such as a school psychologist
- At the discretion of the parent or school, other individuals who have knowledge or special expertise regarding the student, such as a speech-language pathologist or a physical therapist
- Whenever appropriate, the student with a disability (list quoted from 34 CFR §300.321)

Please remember that each member of the IEP team contributes unique and essential information. Parents may be intimidated by the IEP process or may feel less qualified than the professionals on the team; however, parents know their children better than anyone else does. The team should seek and value parental input throughout the IEP process.

How do I work with culturally and linguistically diverse students and their families in the IEP process?

Culturally and linguistically diverse (CLD) students and their families have particular needs that should be addressed throughout the IEP process. The team should understand families' experiences and values related to education, and team members should use this understanding as they identify and evaluate the disability, develop the IEP, and make decisions regarding placement and service provision for the child.

Although the number of CLD students increases annually, most teachers in the United States "remain upper middle class, middle-age, English speaking, and White" (Dyches, Carter, & Prater, 2011, p. 5). Understanding the students' family and cultural contexts will help the team alleviate some of the risk factors related to dropping out of school, failing to graduate, and being inappropriately referred for special education. However, educators must avoid applying general lists of cultural behaviors and attitudes to specific families; such information should merely provide a framework for better understanding and serving these students (Westby, 2009).

Many resources provide helpful suggestions for serving CLD students with disabilities. The following list includes a few points to consider:

- During the evaluation process, be aware that standardized assessment processes and tools may not be designed for use with CLD students.

- Consider contextual factors such as the values, behaviors, and beliefs of the student and his or her family, particularly in the classification process; people from various backgrounds and cultures do not necessarily view disability from the same perspectives as school personnel do.

- Facilitate participation of CLD parents in the IEP process by reducing barriers caused by language and cultural differences, parents' lack of knowledge about the school system, and parents' fear of being told only what is wrong with their child.

- Consider including a cultural mediator in the IEP meetings to (1) translate the discussion and paperwork for parents who do not speak the language of the school professionals and (2) clarify possible misunderstandings due to the culture of the school environment versus that of the student's family.

- Ensure that IEP goals and objectives address both academic and social interaction skills, and acknowledge behaviors that are valued in the student's home and community.

- When determining services and education placement, consider the student's need to access instruction in her or his native language.

CULTURAL AND LINGUISTIC DIFFERENCES

Terms and concepts do not easily translate from one language or culture to another. For instance, in Mexico *educación* includes being moral, responsible, and a *persona de bien*, or "a good person," one who is loyal to family and traditional values (Gallimore & Goldenberg, 2001). Contrast this with the American concept of education, meaning mastery of certain skills and content within an established curriculum. It is not likely that terms used by special educators in the United States will be self-evident when translated for speakers of other languages.

Following the IEP meeting, provide parents with information on relevant community resources and offer them opportunities to interact with other CLD parents of children with disabilities.

Are IEPs created on paper or on a computer?

Both. IEPs can be written on paper forms, but schools and districts increasingly use Web-based IEP management programs. Several companies offer these subscription programs, which generally require an annual fee and then charge by the number of teachers using the program, the number of IEPs, or both. Most IEP management systems can customize forms for states, districts, or schools for an additional fee. Regardless of the format, all IEPs must contain the information required by law, as outlined in this guide.

BE CAREFUL TO USE LANGUAGE THAT PARENTS AND OTHER LAYPEOPLE WILL UNDERSTAND. THE USE OF ACRONYMS AND TECHNICAL LANGUAGE CAN BE CONFUSING.

Who has access to the IEP?

Only parents and authorized school and district personnel may access a student's IEP and other education records that identify the student. IDEA uses the Family Educational Rights and Privacy Act (FERPA) definition of *education records:* "records, files, documents, and other materials maintained by an educational agency or institution, or by a person acting for such an agency or institution, that contain information directly related to a student" (20 USC S. 1232g[a]4A). IDEA requires schools to maintain a record of access, available to the public, on which authorized people must record their name, position, date, and reason for accessing confidential materials. Parents may request copies of a student's IEP and other confidential information, as defined by FERPA.

The law's careful description of access rights has two purposes: (1) it defines who can see information which identifies the student; (2) it informs schools and parents that this information is *confidential,* which means that unauthorized people do not have access to it. For IEP team members, strict confidentiality is required regarding students served by special education. Team members may not disclose such information to others, spoken or written, in or outside school.

Perhaps you have heard an account of a teacher standing in line at a grocery store complaining to a friend about the trials of working with a particular student with a disability. Unnoticed by the teacher, of course, was the student's mother, who happened to be the next person in line and who promptly reported the teacher's breach of confidentiality to the school and district. The lesson from this episode is that teachers must share confidential information *only* with authorized people at appropriate times and in appropriate settings.

How does the team prepare for an IEP meeting?

Preparation depends on whether the student has an existing IEP. Before referring the child to assess a possible disability, the general classroom teacher attempts to address the student's needs by making adaptations or accommodations in the classroom and documents the student's response, showing that these efforts have not been successful in addressing the student's needs. The student's eligibility for special education is based on the resulting assessment. If the student is eligible, the team will develop the initial IEP.

Whether or not the IEP is the child's first, the team prepares for the meeting by collecting the formal and informal assessment data that describe the student's present levels of academic achievement and functional performance. The school representatives and the parents set a mutually agreeable time and place to meet, and the school provides the parents with a written prior notice of the meeting. Sometimes school personnel choose to provide parents with a list of potential goals in advance of the meeting and to invite parents to suggest additional goals.

What happens during an IEP meeting?

Usually the team members meet around a table in a room or office where confidential information can be shared. One of the school professionals conducts the meeting and introduces the participants. If an IEP is currently in place, the team discusses the student's progress toward or achievement of the previous annual goals. The team members then choose whether to continue the existing IEP, revise it, or write a new one. The format of IEP meetings may vary among schools and districts, but the general procedures are the same.

Writing IEPs improves with practice, but a set of steps for completing this important process can be useful to beginners. We have been surprised that many IEPs include the legally required components but are formatted to start at the wrong place in the process: They begin by specifying the services the student will receive instead of by examining the student's current school performance. Thus, IEP teams are inclined to decide special education placement and services before discerning what the student can and needs to do to improve—a classic case of putting the cart before the horse.

What should the team do if a parent cannot or will not attend the IEP meeting?

If a parent cannot attend the meeting, even after good-faith attempts to schedule a mutually agreeable date and time, the law requires the school to use alternative methods of participation, such as videoconferencing or conference calls. If the parent or guardian is unwilling or unable to attend the meeting, the school must maintain a record of its attempts to ensure participation. For example, some districts require the team to send the IEP meeting notice by certified mail so that the mail receipt is a record of the attempt. IDEA also allows the school to email notices if parents choose this option (34 CFR §300.505).

What happens if a team member disagrees with the group's decisions for the IEP?

Sometimes a team member or members may disagree with the final version of an IEP. When parents disagree with other team members, the law provides a mediation process to address concerns. The school or district must ensure that this process is voluntary for all parties, is conducted by a trained and impartial mediator, and is not used to deny or delay parental rights to further due process. A resolution obtained through mediation must result in a legally binding agreement signed by the disputing parties.

The law also allows the school or district to establish other procedures if the parents choose not to use mediation. This alternate choice involves the use of a third-party dispute resolution entity or a parent training or resource center to explain the benefits of mediation. Parents may then choose whether to use mediation to resolve the differences (34 CFR §300.506).

What if mediation doesn't solve the problem?

IDEA guarantees the right of parents or schools to legal due process to resolve disputes relating to a child's identification, evaluation, educational placement, and/or services. Therefore, if mediation does not resolve the concern, parents or schools may request a due process hearing in which legal counsel can call expert witnesses and introduce evidence. A request for due process must be filed within two years of the disputed action. If a due process hearing does not resolve the concern, then both parties have the right to appeal to state or federal courts (34 CFR §300.507).

THE TERM **DUE PROCESS** COMES FROM THE U.S. CONSTITUTION AND MEANS THAT INDIVIDUALS HAVE THE RIGHT TO FULL PROTECTION UNDER THE LAW.

How do teachers and other service providers use the IEP?

Teachers organize instruction to address the IEP goals within the service pattern described, while monitoring student progress toward the attainment of his or her goals. To do this requires that teachers and related service providers carefully plan and implement instruction or intervention and that they collect and use data related to student success. For example, a teacher might state this annual goal for math: "Given 20 multiplication and division problems within 100, Sammy will compute and write the correct answers to 19 of 20 in one trial." Sammy's teacher must analyze the goal to determine what concepts and skills are required to achieve it, then design and conduct a sequence of daily lessons to bring Sammy to this level. The challenge is to determine how much can be taught and measured in the time allowed for daily instruction or intervention that will lead to achieving the goal.

How are IEP progress data collected and used?

Data are collected when teachers or related service providers work from measurable goals or objectives with methods in place to measure student progress regularly. For example, Sammy's teacher should include an assessment of learning for each lesson. If the lesson requires that he compute and write the answer to three multiplication and three matching division problems within 10, then the lesson should include those six items for Sammy to complete during independent practice (see Figure 2). The teacher will record Sammy's score and decide if he has met the mastery criterion. If he has not, more instruction or practice is indicated. Over time the teacher will have a record of the student's progress toward and eventual accomplishment of the annual goal.

Figure 2. Assessing Sammy's math learning.

Name: _____   Date: _____

Write the answers to these problems.

$3 \times 3 =$	$2 \times 5 =$	$3 \times 2 =$
$10 \div 5 =$	$9 \div 3 =$	$6 \div 2 =$

Learning target: Compute and write the answer to three multiplication and three matching division problems within 10.

Is IEP paperwork as time consuming as I have heard it is?

Yes and no. Special education requires more documentation per student served than is necessary for students without disabilities. Special educators are responsible for complying with federal, state, and district law and policy, and compliance must be documented. Just as important, student achievement data inform instructional decisions.

Just know that your approach to maintaining the required documents helps to determine how much time the process consumes. Efficiency makes the difference. You will save the most time if you complete all required documents correctly and in order *the first time* and keep them in an orderly and accessible storage system.

TEACHERS WHO SCRAMBLE TO GATHER INFORMATION AND COMPLETE DOCUMENTS IN PREPARATION FOR AN IEP MEETING, A PROGRAM AUDIT, OR A COMPLIANCE REVIEW CONSUME MUCH MORE TIME THAN THOSE WHO ESTABLISH AND FOLLOW SYSTEMATIC PROCEDURES ALONG THE WAY.

What steps are involved in developing an IEP?

We have outlined seven steps that can lead your team through the process of developing quality IEPs.

1 Describe the student's present levels of academic achievement.

2 Write measurable annual goals.

3 Measure and report student progress.

4 State the services needed to achieve annual goals.

5 Explain the extent, if any, to which the student will not participate with nondisabled students in the regular class and in extracurricular and other nonacademic activities.

6 Explain accommodations necessary to measure academic achievement and functional performance on state and districtwide assessments.

7 Complete a transition plan for students age 16 and older.

When these steps are completed, all IEP team members confirm their participation in the meeting by signing and dating the IEP.

How does the team follow the steps in the IEP process?

You will find a rationale and explanation for each of the steps in this guide so that you can complete the process knowledgeably and professionally. You will also see examples from four case studies of students with disabilities and, where appropriate, counterexamples to guide your learning and help you discriminate between correct and incorrect procedures. Then you will practice each of the steps to check your understanding. As you complete each self-check exercise, compare your answers with our suggested answers in the appendix.

YOU ARE READY TO GO! ENJOY YOUR LEARNING, AND MAY YOU FIND SUCCESS AND FULFILLMENT AS YOU CREATE IEPS FOR THESE MARVELOUS CHILDREN.

References

Dyches, T. T., Carter, N., & Prater, M. A. (2011). *A teacher's guide to communicating with parents: Practical strategies for developing successful relationships.* Needham Heights, MA: Pearson/Allyn & Bacon.

Family Educational Right to Privacy Act (1988). 53 FR 11943, 20 USC S. 1232g. Retrieved from www.ecfr.gov/cgi-bin/text-idx?c=ecfr&sid=11975031b82001bed902b3e73f33e604&rgn=div5&view=text&node=34:1.1.1.1.33&idno=34

Gallimore, R., & Goldenberg, C. (2001). Analyzing cultural models and settings to connect minority achievement and school improvement research. *Educational Psychologist, 36*(1), 45–56. doi:10.1207/S15326985EP3601_5

Office of Special Education Programs. (2000). *Twenty-five years of progress in educating children with disabilities through IDEA.* Washington, DC: Author. Retrieved from www2.ed.gov/policy/speced/leg/idea/history.pdf

Rehabilitation Act of 1973. Pub. L. No. 93-112, 87 Stat. 355. 29 U.S.C. §§ 701–796. Retrieved from www.usbr.gov/cro/pdfsplus/rehabact.pdf

U.S. Department of Education Assistance to States for the Education of Children with Disabilities and Preschool Grants for Children with Disabilities; Final Rule, 34 CFR Parts 300, 301, and Part C§636 (2006). Retrieved from www.ed.gov/policy/speced/guid/idea/idea2004.html#law

Warren, M. P., & Kirkendall, D. (1973). *Bottom high to the crowd.* New York, NY: Walker.

Westby, C. (2009). Considerations in working successfully with culturally/linguistically diverse families in assessment and intervention of communication disorders. *Seminars in Speech and Language, 30*(4), 279–289.

Meet Our Students

We would like you become acquainted with four students of various ages and types of disabilities, each with a brief biography and an individualized education program (IEP). We believe the biographies remind educators that students are people with their own unique circumstances, not just names on documents. So much of what influences a student's life and learning occurs outside the classroom and the school day; teachers who understand this are more likely to teach the whole child.

The IEPs are examples based on our experience and understanding of the required components described in the Individuals with Disabilities Education Improvement Act (IDEA). You may notice variations in document formats, indicating that state or district IEPs may differ in appearance or organization while still containing the necessary components.

Our students are

- Jameelah, an eighth-grade girl with specific learning disabilities living in an urban area

- Ricky, a fifth-grade boy with serious emotional disturbance living in a small community

- Spencer, a 7-year-old boy with autism who learns from an alternate curriculum

- Angelica, a 20-year-old woman with intellectual disability preparing for transition to postschool life

JAMEELAH BRADLEY

Jameelah Bradley is an eighth-grade African American girl served in special education for specific learning disabilities at Woodrow Wilson Middle School. The school is an older building situated in a rundown area of a midsize Northeast city. The school population is primarily African American with a mix of Latino and Vietnamese students from traditionally working-class neighborhoods with above-average unemployment.

Family and Cultural Background

Jameelah lives with her father, his companion Tamika, and her younger brother in a subsidized apartment within walking distance of the school. Her father is a bus driver for the city's transit system and has a second job on weekends as a security guard at a local amusement center for youth. Jameelah's father and Tamika are raising the children without assistance from either the father's or Tamika's extended family, and they try to make home life as stable as possible. Mr. Bradley struggled with an undiagnosed learning disability in reading and didn't graduate from high school. He has since learned to value formal education and supports and encourages his children in their academic endeavors. Tamika graduated from high school and finished two years of postsecondary education to earn a medical assisting degree, but she is not currently employed. She does most of the homework tutoring in the family.

Jameelah spends her free time with two female friends. They are all in the school orchestra, sing in the school choir, and enjoy watching televised talent contests.

School Experience

Jameelah seemed to do well in school until the last half of second grade, when it became evident that she lagged behind her peers in reading achievement. Her teacher encouraged Mr. Bradley to read with her at home, but no improvement resulted. Midway through the next year, her third-grade teacher discussed the matter with a resource teacher and decided to refer Jameelah for evaluation. Even though the teacher had not implemented evidence-based remedial practices, the local education agency (LEA) representative accepted the referral and the child study team completed eligibility assessment. Jameelah began receiving specialized reading instruction in the resource room for 40 minutes each day.

Her sixth-grade teacher realized that Jameelah was falling behind in math, even with extra help, and brought the matter to the attention of the IEP team. Following appropriate evaluation, the team added specialized instruction in math to her IEP.

Jameelah does not exhibit behaviors that interfere with her progress or the progress of other students in her classes. She attends school regularly and gets along well with her peers and her teachers.

INDIVIDUALIZED EDUCATION PROGRAM

1. Student Information

Student _Jameelah Bradley_   3-Year Reevaluation _2/12/_   Date of Birth _5/05/_

School _Wilson Middle_   IEP Meeting _2/11/_   Classification _Specific learning disabilities_

IEP Due _2/12/_   Grade _8_   Initial Eligibility _2/12/_

2. Present Levels of Academic Achievement and Functional Performance

Reading

Informal passage fluency measures (1/21/__) show Jameelah has mastered oral reading standards to the fifth-grade level but cannot read sixth- or seventh-grade passages fluently. _Woodcock-Johnson Tests of Achievement_ (1/28/__) indicate she has mastered passage comprehension standards to fifth-grade level, but she cannot comprehend accurately at the sixth-grade level or beyond. To progress in the eighth-grade general curriculum, Jameelah needs to read and comprehend literature, including stories, dramas, and poems, at the high end of the grades 6 to 8 text complexity band independently and proficiently (CCSS.ELA-LITERACY.RI.8.10).*

*CCSS stands for Common Core State Standards.

Math

KeyMath-3 (1/21/___) shows Jameelah has mastered math standards to the fifth-grade level. She cannot explain the value of irrational numbers, perform operations in scientific notation, or solve problems using linear equations with two variables. Jameelah needs to use rational approximations of irrational numbers to compare the size of irrational numbers, locate them approximately on a number line, and estimate the value of expressions (CCSS.MATH.CONTENT.8.NS.A.2); perform operations with numbers expressed in scientific notation, including problems where both decimal and scientific notation are used (CCSS.MATH.CONTENT.8.EE.A.4); and solve real-world and mathematical problems leading to two linear equations in two variables (CCSS.MATH.CONTENT.8.EE.C.8.C).

3. Measurable Annual Goals

Reading

1. _Given stories, dramas, and poems of eighth-grade complexity read aloud to her and weekly opportunities to practice, Jameelah will say or write answers to literal and inferential questions about theme, characters, and events with at least 90% accuracy on two samples of each text type, as measured by teacher observation records and informal written work (CCSS.ELA-LITERACY.RI.8.10)._

2. _Given reading passages at the seventh-grade level from fiction, nonfiction, and poetry, and weekly opportunities to practice, Jameelah will orally read each text type at 100 or more words correct per minute with at least 95% accuracy in four of five opportunities as measured by progress monitoring and teacher observation records._

3. _Given reading passages at the seventh-grade level from fiction, nonfiction, and poetry, and weekly opportunities to practice, Jameelah will read the passages and say or write answers to literal and inferential comprehension questions with at least 80% accuracy for four of five passages as measured by teacher observation records._

Math

4. *Given numbers such as 3, 5.3, 1.7, $\pi/2$, $\sqrt{10}$ and daily opportunities to practice, Jameelah will place them on a number line with at least 80% accuracy as measured by written work (CCSS.MATH.CONTENT.8.NS.A.2).*

5. *Given problems using scientific notation, such as $(2 \times 10^3)(2 \times 10^4)$ or $.02^2$ and daily opportunities to practice, Jameelah will compute answers with at least 90% accuracy as measured by written work (CCSS.MATH.CONTENT.8.EE.A.4).*

6. *Given real-world problems leading to two linear equations in two variables, such as when given coordinates for two pairs of points, she must determine whether the line through the first pair of points intersects the line through the second pair, and weekly opportunities to practice, Jameelah will write answers with at least 90% accuracy as measured by written work (CCSS.MATH.CONTENT.8.EE.C.8.C).*

4. The IEP Team Considered the Following Special Factors

Behavior	Not needed.
Language	Not needed.
Braille	Not needed.
Communication	Not needed.
Assistive technology	Not needed.

5. Special Education and Related Services Needed to Progress in the General Curriculum

Special Education Service	Location	Time/Frequency
Small-group reading	Special education class	50 min 5 × weekly

Related Service
None

Program modifications, supports for school personnel, and/or supplementary aids in the regular education program
None

6. Participation in State and District Assessment

Participation Codes

S	Standard administration	No accommodations or modifications
A	Participate with accommodations	Does not invalidate, alter, or lower standard
M	Participate with modifications	Invalidates, alters, or lowers standard
AA	Participate using alternate assessment: ☐ Out-of-level criterion-referenced test (CRT) ☐ State alternate assessment	Aligned more closely with alternate curriculum than regular curriculum

	Accommodations	Criterion-Referenced Tests (CRTs)			Direct Writing Assessment	State High School Competency Test		
		Language Arts	Math	Science		Reading	Writing	Math
Presentation	1. Directions read aloud in English	A	A	A				
	2. Questions read aloud in English		A	A		No		
	3. Directions signed							
	4. Questions signed					No		
	5. Screen reader					No		
	6. Directions—oral translation							
	7. Questions—oral translation	No			No	No	No	
	8. Large print							
	9. Magnification devices							
	10. Braille							
	11. Tactile graphics							
	12. Audio amplification devices							
	13. Visual cues							
	14. Talking materials							
	15. Bilingual word lists	—	—	—	—			
	16. Translated formulas	—		—	—	—	—	
Response	17. Word processor—no spell check		—	—				—
	18. Calculation devices	—			—	—	—	
	19. Write in test booklet							
	20. Scribe							
	21. Visual organizers							
	22. Graphic organizers							
	23. Speech-to-text conversion							
	24. Brailler							
	25. Recording device							
Setting	26. Reduce distractions to student							
	27. Reduce distractions to others							
	28. Physical access							
Timing	29. Extended time							
	30. Multiple breaks							
	31. Schedule change							
Other	32. Other: Temporary (504 only)							

No: Accommodations not allowed

—: Not applicable

7. Regular Curriculum, Extracurricular, and Nonacademic Activities

The student will participate in the regular class and in extracurricular and other nonacademic activities except as noted in special education and related services, or listed here:

8. Schedule for Written IEP Progress Reports to Parents

	Weekly	Biweekly	Monthly	Quarterly	Semiannually
Home note					
Progress report				X	
Parent conference					X
Report card				X	
Other					

9. Transition Plan (IEP Beginning the Year the Student Turns 16, or before if Applicable)

Not applicable

10. Special Requirements for Graduation

Not applicable

11. Notices and Participants

Extended School Year (ESY): ESY services are provided when the team determines the student requires services beyond the normal school year for the provision of free appropriate public education.
☐ Student is eligible for ESY.
☒ Student is not eligible for ESY.

Placement Review
☐ Initial placement   ☒ Continue placement   ☐ Change placement

IEP Team Participants

Position	Name	Signature	Date
LEA representative	Martin Feldhauser	*Martin Feldhauser*	2/11/____
Special education teacher	Vicky Ulloa	*Vicky Ulloa*	2/11/____
Regular education teacher	Bob Fisher	*Bob Fisher*	2/11/____
Student	Jameelah Bradley	*Jameelah Bradley*	2/11/____
Parent	John Bradley	*John Bradley*	2/11/____
Speech-language pathologist			
Translator			
Other related service provider(s)			

RICKY LOPEZ

Ricky Lopez is a first generation Mexican American fifth-grade boy being served in special education for severe emotional disturbance at Dry Mesa Elementary School in a suburban Southwest community. The school has a mix of Caucasian, Hispanic, and Native American students from lower- to middle-class neighborhoods.

Family and Cultural Background

Ricky lives with his widowed mother and older sister in a generally peaceful subdivision. His mother and father emigrated from Mexico as a young married couple, but his father died in a construction accident shortly after Ricky was born. His mother earns an adequate living as an office manager for a multilingual community outreach program and is grateful that her family has the necessities and a little extra. The family speaks primarily Spanish in the home, but the children also speak fluent conversational English learned through their school and neighborhood experiences. Ricky's mother has taught her children about Mexican culture, and they usually gather with friends from the Mexican American community to celebrate important days. Mother did well in high school but has not had the time or money to pursue her goal to complete a degree in business management.

Ricky spends his free time drawing distorted battle creatures in his room or roaming the neighborhood with his only friend, a boy who is several years older and seldom attends school. Mother worries about the older boy's influence on Ricky's thoughts and actions.

School Experience

Ricky was a quiet kindergartner who started school with no grasp of English. He easily imitated other children but understood little of what the teacher said. His language skills improved over time through the school's services for English language learners, and by the middle of first grade he was conversing and learning to read and write in English. In second grade, he began to lag behind his peers in class participation, assignment completion, and playground interactions. In early third grade, he began defying his male teacher and exhibiting violent outbursts when frustrated, typified by tearing papers, throwing his book or pencil, or pounding on the computer keyboard. When reprimanded by the teacher, he sulked and refused to comply with directives or to respond to conversational prompts. His angry periods lasted longer and longer until, by the end of the year, he took an hour or more to return to a reasonable state. His female fourth-grade teacher was kind and patient, but Ricky's noncompliance and anger outbursts continued. At this time, he received an average of one office disciplinary referral per week. By November, the teacher and principal agreed to refer him for evaluation by the special education team. His mother granted permission, and the assessment was completed by the school psychologist and a resource teacher. Results indicated that Ricky was eligible for special education services for severe emotional disturbance, which began in fourth grade.

Relevant Academic and Behavioral Information

Ricky manifests frustration when he must wait his turn in the cafeteria or on the playground by pushing other students or trying to take their places in line. He expresses his frustration with reading by refusing to open his book, pushing books off his desk, or angrily refusing to initiate independent assignments. He will not read aloud in class, even at his comfort level; therefore, it is difficult for his teacher to know how much he understands. He attends a resource class for reading help and has a good relationship with his special education teacher. His IEP team is working on decreasing behavior outbursts in the classroom and cafeteria, and increasing his time on task for class work involving reading.

Ricky does well in math but struggles in reading. His penmanship is poor but passable. He takes interest in science labs, computer simulations, and other hands-on activities. Dynamic Indicators of Basic Early Literacy Skills (DIBELS)© oral reading fluency assessment indicates that he reads fifth-grade-level passages at 52 words correct per minute with 74% accuracy, but he should be reading 120 or more words correct per minute with 98% accuracy. When tested on other grade-level passages, his reading matched the oral reading fluency benchmarks for words correct per minute and accuracy at the beginning third-grade level. His IEP team has determined that his classroom behaviors, including his resistance to participating in reading activities and practice, significantly affect his achievement.

INDIVIDUALIZED EDUCATION PROGRAM

1. Student Information

Student *Ricky Lopez*

DOB *6/04/*

IEP Meeting *10/22/*

IEP Due *10/28/*

3-Year Reevaluation *10/23/*

School *Dry Mesa Elementary*

Classification *Serious emotional disturbance*

Grade *5* Eligibility Date *10/24/*

2. Present Levels of Academic Achievement and Functional Performance

Reading

DIBELS oral reading fluency testing (10/08/__) indicates that Ricky has met standards through third grade for reading fluency and comprehension, but he cannot read or comprehend at fourth-grade standards. Ricky needs to read with sufficient accuracy and fluency to support comprehension at the sixth-grade level to progress in the general curriculum (CCSS.ELA-Literacy.RF.5.4).

Behavior

During three 30-minute classroom observations (9/15/__, 9/17/__, 9/23/__), Ricky refused to comply with teacher requests or directives an average of seven out of seven times and pushed reading materials away or off his desk an average of three out of three times. During two 15-minute cafeteria observations (9/16, 10/18) Ricky had two instances each of pushing students out of line, cutting in the food and tray deposit lines, and verbally refusing an adult's reminders that these behaviors are against the rules. Ricky needs to decrease behavior outbursts in the classroom and cafeteria and to increase compliance with teacher directives to interact appropriately with others to progress in the general curriculum.

3. The IEP Team Considered the Following Special Factors

Behavior	Ricky needs behavioral strategies because his behavior impedes his learning and/or the learning of others.
Language	Ricky needs continued services through the school's English as a Second Language program.
Braille	Not needed.
Communication	Not needed.
Assistive technology	Not needed.

4. Measurable Annual Goals

Reading

1. *Given three sixth-grade reading passages read orally, Ricky will listen and say or write answers to literal and inferential comprehension questions with at least 95% accuracy, as measured by student work samples and teacher observation records.*
2. *Given three fifth-grade fiction and nonfiction passages, Ricky will read aloud at 130 words correct per minute with at least 95% accuracy, as measured by DIBELS Oral Reading Fluency.*

Behavior

1. *When requested or directed by the teacher, Ricky will comply without removing materials for at least 90% of opportunities in any class period over 5 days, as measured by student self-monitoring and teacher observation records.*

2. *When in the cafeteria, Ricky will take his place in line and remain there without pushing or otherwise removing other students for 100% of opportunities, as measured by observer tallies 3 times in one week.*

5. Special Education and Related Services Needed to Progress in the General Curriculum

Service	Location	Time	Frequency	Begin Date	Duration
Reading fluency and comprehension	Regular Class **Special Class** Other:	*45 min*	**Daily** Weekly Monthly	*9/16*	**1 year** Other:

Service	Location	Time	Frequency	Begin Date	Duration
Behavior intervention	Regular Class Special Class **Other:** **School psychology office**	*20 min*	**Daily** **Weekly** *2x* Monthly	*9/16*	**1 year** Other:

Program modifications, supports for school personnel, and or supplementary aids in the regular education program
School psychologist will consult with general education teacher to teach and model
behavior data collection and positive reinforcement in the classroom.

6. Participation in State and District Assessment

Participation Codes

S	Standard administration	No accommodations or modifications
A	Participate with accommodations	Does not invalidate, alter, or lower standard
M	Participate with modifications	Invalidates, alters, or lowers standard
AA	Participate using alternate assessment: ☐ Out-of-level criterion-referenced test (CRT) ☐ State alternate assessment	Aligned more closely with alternate curriculum than regular curriculum

		Criterion Referenced Tests				State High School Competency Test		
	Accommodations	Language Arts	Math	Science	Direct Writing Assessment	Reading	Writing	Math
Presentation	1. Directions read aloud in English		A	A		A		
	2. Questions read aloud in English					No		
	3. Directions signed							
	4. Questions signed					No		
	5. Screen reader					No		
	6. Directions—oral translation							

	Accommodations	Criterion Referenced Tests			Direct Writing Assessment	State High School Competency Test		
		Language Arts	Math	Science		Reading	Writing	Math
Presentation	7. Questions—oral translation	No			No	No	No	
	8. Large print							
	9. Magnification deices							
	10. Braille							
	11. Tactile graphics							
	12. Audio amplification devices							
	13. Visual cues							
	14. Talking materials							
	15. Bilingual word lists	—	—	—	—			
	16. Translated formulas	—		—	—	—	—	
Response	17. Word processor—no spell check		—	—				—
	18. Calculation devices	—			—	—	—	
	19. Write in test booklet							
	20. Scribe							
	21. Visual organizers							
	22. Graphic organizers							
	23. Speech-to-text conversion							
	24. Brailler							
	25. Recording device							
Setting	26. Reduce distractions to student							
	27. Reduce distractions to others							
	28. Physical access							
Timing	29. Extended time							
	30. Multiple breaks							
	31. Schedule change							
Other	32. Other: Temporary (504 only)							

No: Accommodations not allowed
—: Not applicable

7. Regular Curriculum, Extracurricular, and Nonacademic Activities
The student will participate in the regular class, and in extracurricular and other nonacademic activities except as noted in special education and related services or listed here: N/A

8. Schedule for Written IEP Progress Reports to Parents

	Weekly	Biweekly	Monthly	Quarterly	Semiannually
Home note					
Progress report			X		
Parent conference					X
Report card				X	
Other					

9. Transition Plan (for IEP Beginning the Year the Student Turns 16, or before if Applicable)

Not applicable

10. Special Requirements for Graduation

Not applicable

11. Notices and Participants

Extended School Year (ESY): ESY services are provided when the team determines the student will not benefit if services are not provided during the normal summer break.

☐ Student is eligible for ESY.

☒ Student is not eligible for ESY.

Placement Review

☐ Initial placement   ☒ Continue placement   ☐ Change placement

IEP Team Participants

Position	Name	Signature	Date
LEA representative	Eduardo Flores	E. D. Flores	10/22/
Special education teacher	Giselle Bachmeier	Giselle Bachmeier	10/22/
Regular education teacher	Anna Espinoza	A. Espinoza	10/22/
Student	Ricky Lopez	Ricky Lopez	10/22/
Parent	Maria Lopez	Maria J. Lopez	10/22/
School psychologist	Marty Goode	MartinF.Goode	10/22/
ESL instructor	Gloria Peres	Gloria Peres	10/22/
Translator			

SPENCER HALL

Spencer Hall is a 7-year-old Caucasian boy educationally classified as having autism.

Family and Cultural Background

Spencer lives at home with a 9-year-old sister, a 4-year-old brother, his mom and dad, and his maternal grandmother. Mr. Hall works as a computer software programmer; Mrs. Hall works part-time as a speech-language pathology (SLP) assistant at Wasden Elementary, which is within walking distance of their home. They are Caucasian and have strong family and religious traditions. Spencer has been accepted by his neighbors and church members, who are actively engaged in learning how to integrate Spencer into the community effectively.

Prior School Experience

Mrs. Hall noticed Spencer's unusual development when he was 18 months old and wondered if he might have autism. Although at times he appeared to be unusually bright, Mrs. Hall was concerned about his poor speech and communication and his unusual play behaviors. She reported to her pediatrician that Spencer often acted like he was deaf or was "in his own world." The pediatrician referred them to a diagnostician specializing in autism spectrum disorders (ASDs), and at age 2, Spencer was diagnosed as having ASD. Mrs. Hall is familiar with students with special needs because of her work as an SLP aide, and she had Spencer evaluated by their local early intervention provider. He received center-based and in-home services until he was 3 years old, then began attending a preschool for students with developmental delays at Wasden Elementary. He attended kindergarten at Wasden in a class for students with developmental delays, was included in a general education classroom during first grade, and has recently begun second grade in a general education classroom with support from a para-educator for 3 hours a day.

Current Schooling

Spencer is currently in the second grade in his neighborhood school, Wasden Elementary, which has 545 students, one principal, and 25 teachers. Spencer's teacher, Ms. Albright, is a third-year teacher of a class of 20 first-grade students, three of whom receive special education services. Ms. Albright works closely with Mr. Bowman, the special educator, to provide the special education services as specified on Spencer's IEP. Ms. Albright is assisted by one part-time para-educator to help all students in the class who need additional assistance, and the para-educator provides frequent individual support to Spencer during math, English/language arts, physical education, recess, and specialty classes (e.g., media center, art, music). He receives speech services through the licensed SLP at the school, who coordinates the integration of services into his school day, provides direct services to Spencer, and provides training related to Spencer's augmentative and alternative communication services.

Ms. Albright reports that Spencer is expected to engage in the same curricular activities as the other second-grade students, but he needs additional instruction and support in communicating effectively, engaging in positive social skills, and replacing his restrictive patterns of behavior with more functional routines and activities. Spencer learns best when he is given realistic expectations, clear visual and verbal directions, and standard functional routines.

INDIVIDUALIZED EDUCATION PROGRAM

Student: _Spencer Hall_ Birth date: _8/10/_ Grade: _Second_

IEP Date: _9/15/_ School: _Wasden Elementary_ Classification: _Autism_

Present Levels of Academic Achievement and Functional Performance

MATH: According to results from the state alternate assessment (September 11), Spencer's math skills are at a kindergarten level (he can accurately identify numbers from 1 to 100, count objects to 10, and identify four basic shapes). He cannot perform many of the prerequisite skills necessary to achieve the second-grade standards. To progress in the general education curriculum, Spencer needs to tell and write time from analog and digital clocks to the nearest 5 minutes (CCSS.Math.Content.2.MD.C.7); use addition and subtraction within 20 (CCSS.Math.Content.2.OA.B.2); and recognize and draw shapes having specified attributes, such as a given number of angles or a given number of equal faces (CCSS.Math.Content.2.G.A.1).

ENGLISH LANGUAGE ARTS: According to the state alternate assessment (September 12), Spencer's reading skills are at a kindergarten level. He can match uppercase and lowercase letters, trace all letters of the alphabet, recognize rhyming words, and select 50 pictures on his communication device. He cannot print letters, write words independently, or perform the prerequisite skills required to meet the second-grade standards. To progress in the general curriculum, he needs to use phonics and word analysis skills in decoding words (CCSS.ELA-Literacy.RF.2.3) and use a variety of digital tools to produce and publish writing (CCSS.ELA-Literacy.W.2.6).

SOCIAL: According to the Social Skills Checklist administered by the special educator (May 15), Spencer can give eye contact when his name is called, follow one-step directions, and respond when others greet him. He can entertain himself for long periods of time with electronic devices, but he cannot currently initiate interactions with his peers. He interacts with others only when they have items that are interesting to him—he often takes those items rather than asking for a turn (on average six times per day). Spencer needs to learn to initiate and engage in positive social interactions with peers without assistance.

COMMUNICATION: According to recent testing by the SLP (September 8), Spencer can communicate with approximately 20 spoken words (e.g., Mom, no, yeah, iPad, want), and use an electronic communication device to communicate many of his other wants and needs (50-word vocabulary). He cannot initiate using social greetings or initiate conversations with peers. Spencer needs to increase his expressive vocabulary, initiate social greetings, and communicate with peers.

BEHAVIOR: According to end-of-year data from Spencer's first-grade teacher, Spencer can attend to tasks for up to 5 minutes, follow picture-based rules without teacher prompting, and follow standard routines. When Spencer is prevented from doing what he wants to do or when transitioning to a different activity, he screams and bites his wrist, which he does on average 10 times per day. Spencer is extremely sensitive to noise and crowds of people; in these situations, he often covers his ears and runs out of the area. Spencer needs to transition without screaming or biting himself and to stay in the learning area alongside his nondisabled peers.

FUNCTIONAL LIFE SKILLS: According to end-of-year data from his special educator and his parents, Spencer can undress and dress himself independently, but he cannot use zippers, snaps, or buttons without prompting. He resists physical prompts to fasten his clothes. Spencer needs to fasten his clothes independently.

Measurable Annual Goals

1. **MATH:** *When assessed on the state alternate assessment at the end of the school year, Spencer will increase his math skills to a 1.6 grade level in at least 80% of the tested subdomains (EE.2.MD.7; EE.1.OA.1; EE.2.G.1).*

Benchmarks/Short-Term Objectives

a. *When given a clock, Spencer will tell the time to the hour, the half hour, and 15-minute increments (using his communication device or verbally) with at least 80% accuracy, with at least two different types of clocks (digital or analog), and maintain the skill when probed weekly for 2 weeks.*

b. *When given addition and subtraction problems within 20, Spencer will solve the problems with at least 80% accuracy, under three different conditions and maintain this skill when probed weekly for 2 weeks.*

c. *When asked to draw a shape (e.g., triangle, quadrilateral, pentagon, hexagon), Spencer will draw the identified shape with at least 80% accuracy, under three different conditions, and maintain this skill when probed weekly for 2 weeks.*

Student's progress toward goal measured by:

☐ formal assessment   ☐ criterion-referenced test   ☐ curriculum-based assessment
☒ checklists   ☐ work samples   ☐ self-monitoring

2. **ENGLISH LANGUAGE ARTS:** *When assessed on the state alternate assessment at the end of the school year, Spencer will increase his reading and writing skills to a 1.6 grade level in at least 80% of the tested subdomains (EE.RF.2.3; EE.R1.2.4; EE.SL.2.1-3; EE.W.2.6).*

Benchmarks/Short-Term Objectives

a. *When asked to find an uppercase or lowercase letter of the alphabet on his communication device, Spencer will correctly point to the designated letter with no more than four mistakes, with at least three different type fonts, and maintain this skill when probed weekly for 2 weeks.*

b. *When presented with 10 pre-primer functional words, Spencer will point to a picture representing each written word, with at least 80% accuracy, using various pictures and type fonts, and maintain this skill when probed weekly for at least 2 weeks.*

c. *When given 32 new pictures on his communication device, Spencer will activate each picture accurately to provide a comment, at least three times a day, and maintain this skill when probed weekly for at least 2 weeks.*

d. *When given a visual model of basic words (e.g., first and last name, reading vocabulary), Spencer will copy the words on his paper or on his communication device with at least 80% correct formation, at least three times each day and maintain this skill when probed weekly for at least 2 weeks.*

Student's progress toward goal measured by:

☐ formal assessment   ☐ criterion-referenced test   ☒ curriculum-based assessment
☐ checklists   ☐ work samples   ☐ self-monitoring

3. **SOCIAL:** *When other children are playing, Spencer will point to the item he wants to play with and say (or activate his communication device) "play," without taking the item from the child, at least 80% of the time, with at least 3 different items and in at least two different settings (free time, recess), and maintain this skill when probed weekly for at least 3 weeks.*

Benchmarks/Short-Term Objectives

a. *In 10 weeks, when children are playing, Spencer will point to the item he wants to play with and say or point to "play" with a **full physical prompt**, without taking the item from the child, at least 80% of the time, with at least 3 different items and in at least 2 different settings (free time, recess) and maintain this skill when probed weekly for at least 3 weeks.*

b. *In 20 weeks, when children are playing, Spencer will point to the item he wants to play with and say or point to "play" with a **partial physical prompt**, without taking the item from the child, at least 80% of the time, with at least 3 different items and in at least 2 different settings (free time, recess) and maintain this skill when probed weekly for at least 3 weeks.*

c. *In 30 weeks, when children are playing, Spencer will point to the item he wants to play with and say or point to "play" with a **teacher model**, without taking the item from the child, at least 80% of the time, with at least 3 different items and in at least 2 different settings (free time, recess) and maintain this skill when probed weekly for at least 3 weeks.*

Student's progress toward goal measured by:
☐ formal assessment ☐ criterion-referenced test ☐ curriculum-based assessment
☒ checklists ☐ work samples ☐ self-monitoring

4. **COMMUNICATION:** *When Spencer approaches a peer, he will use speech or his communication device to make a social greeting and engage in a 1-minute conversation, at least 80% of observed occurrences, with at least two different people in at least two different settings, and maintain this skill when probed weekly for 2 weeks.*

Benchmarks/Short-Term Objectives

a. *When Spencer approaches a peer, he will **greet** the person in at least 80% of observed occurrences, with at least two different people in two different settings, and maintain this skill when probed weekly for 2 weeks.*

b. *After exchanging greetings with a peer, Spencer will **ask questions and respond** to the peer's questions for 1 minute (using speech or his communication device) in at least 80% of observed occurrences, with at least two different people in two different settings, and maintain this skill when probed weekly for 2 weeks.*

Student's progress toward goal measured by:
☐ formal assessment ☐ criterion-referenced test ☐ curriculum-based assessment
☒ checklists ☐ work samples ☐ self-monitoring

5. **BEHAVIOR:** *When asked to stop an activity or to change activities and when presented with a visual schedule of the upcoming activity, Spencer will take the visual schedule (and any necessary materials) to the next activity with zero occurrences of screaming or biting his wrist, over three different conditions, and he will maintain this skill when probed weekly for three consecutive weeks.*

Benchmarks/Short-Term Objectives

a. *When asked to stop an activity or to change activities and when presented with a visual schedule of the upcoming activity, Spencer will take the visual schedule (and any necessary materials) to the next activity, with **fewer than six (6)** occurrences of screaming or biting his wrist, over three different conditions, and he will maintain this skill when probed weekly for 3 consecutive weeks.*

b. *When asked to stop an activity or to change activities and when presented with a visual schedule of the upcoming activity, Spencer will take the visual schedule (and any necessary materials) to the next activity, with **fewer than three (3)** occurrences of screaming or biting his wrist, over three different conditions, and he will maintain this skill when probed weekly for 3 consecutive weeks.*

Student's progress toward goal measured by:

☐ formal assessment   ☐ criterion-referenced test   ☐ curriculum-based assessment
☒ checklists   ☐ work samples   ☐ self-monitoring

6. **FUNCTIONAL LIFE SKILLS:** *When Spencer needs to fasten his clothes (e.g., after using the restroom, when putting on his coat), he will correctly fasten his clothes within 1 minute with no prompts, four out of five times weekly with at least three different fasteners (e.g., snaps, zippers, buttons), and maintain this skill when probed weekly for 2 consecutive weeks.*

Benchmarks/Short-Term Objectives

a. *When his clothes are unzipped, Spencer will correctly **zip** them within 1 minute, four out of five times without prompting, with at least two different items of clothing, and he will maintain this skill when probed weekly for 2 consecutive weeks.*

b. *When his clothes are not snapped, Spencer will correctly **snap** them within 1 minute, four out of five times without prompting, with at least two different items of clothing, and he will maintain this skill when probed weekly for 2 consecutive weeks.*

c. *When his clothes are not buttoned, Spencer will correctly **button** them within 1 minute, four out of five times without prompting, with at least two different items of clothing, and he will maintain this skill when probed weekly for 2 consecutive weeks.*

Student's progress toward goal measured by:

☐ formal assessment   ☐ criterion-referenced test   ☐ curriculum-based assessment
☒ checklists   ☐ work samples   ☐ self-monitoring

Special Education Services to Achieve Annual Goals and Advance in General Curriculum

Service	Location	Time	Frequency	Begin Date	Duration
Specially designed instruction	**Regular Class** Special Class Other:	3 hrs	**Daily** Weekly Monthly	9/16	**1 year** Other:
Specially designed instruction	Regular Class **Special Class** Other:	3 hrs	**Daily** Weekly Monthly	9/16	**1 year** Other:

Related Services to Benefit from Special Education

Service	Location	Time	Frequency	Begin Date	Duration
Speech-language services	Regular Class Special Class **Other:** **Therapy Room**	20 min	**Daily** Weekly Monthly	9/16	**1 year** Other:

Program Modifications and/or Supplementary Aids and Services in Regular Classes

Modifications/Personnel Support	Frequency	Supplementary Aids and Services	Frequency
Autism training; positive behavior support training and consultation	Daily Weekly **Monthly**	Personal communication device	**Daily** Weekly Monthly

Applicable Special Factors

Factor	Not Needed	In IEP
Positive behavior instruction and support when behavior impedes learning of student or others		✓
Language needs for student with limited English proficiency	✓	
Braille instruction for student who is blind or visually impaired	✓	
Communication and/or language services for student who is deaf, is hard of hearing, or has other communication needs		✓
Assistive technology devices or services		✓

Participation in Regular Class, Extracurricular, and Nonacademic Activities

The student will participate in the regular class and in extracurricular and other nonacademic activities except as noted in special education and related services or listed here:

Spencer will not participate in lunch in the cafeteria at the same time as other students or in in-school assemblies. Due to his need to have intensive, individualized instruction in a quiet environment, he will not participate in some regular class instruction.

Schedule for Written IEP Progress Reports to Parents

	Weekly	Biweekly	Monthly	Quarterly	Semiannually
Home note	X				
Progress report			X		
Parent conference					X
Report card				X	
Other					

Transition Plan

Complete and attach for students age 16 and older.
Not applicable

Participation in State and District Assessments

Participation Codes

S	Standard administration	No accommodations or modifications
A	Participate with accommodations	Does not invalidate, alter, or lower standard
M	Participate with modifications	Invalidates, alters, or lowers standard
AA	Participate using alternate assessment: ☐ Out-of-level criterion-referenced test ☒ State alternate assessment	Aligned more closely with alternate curriculum than general education curriculum

State and District Assessment Matrix

Enter appropriate participation code for each applicable assessment.

Grade	Kindergarten Pretest	Kindergarten Post-Test	State Criterion-Referenced Math	State Criterion-Referenced Language Arts	State Criterion-Referenced Science	Iowa Test of Basic Skills	National Assessment Educational Progress
K							
1							
2			AA	AA	AA	AA	AA
3							
4							
5							
6							
7							
8							
9							
10							
11							
12							

Accommodations and Modifications

List specific accommodations and modifications for assessments.
Not applicable

Alternate Assessment

State why student cannot participate in regular assessment.
Spencer's skills in math and language arts are approximately 1 to 2 years behind his nondisabled peers; his poor communication skills, limited attention span, and inability to write impair his ability to demonstrate his achievement successfully on standardized tests.

State why selected alternate assessment is appropriate.
Spencer was administered the state alternate assessment at the beginning of this year and was able to demonstrate his skills, given multiple testing breaks, prompts to stay on task, concrete examples, and multiple explanations of the tasks, in a one-on-one setting.

Special Requirements for Graduation

Not applicable

Extended School Year

Extended school year (ESY) services are provided when the team determines the student requires special education and related services beyond the normal school year.

☒ Student is eligible for ESY.
☐ Student is not eligible for ESY.

Placement Review

☐ Initial placement   ☒ Continue placement   ☐ Change placement

IEP Team Participants

Whitney Hall	Parent
Larry Hall	Parent
MaryRoseDurkee	LEA representative
Jamey Albright	Regular class teacher
Barry Bowman	Special education teacher
LANCE WILCOX	School psychologist
Tonya Gottschalk	Speech-language pathologist

If parent signature is missing, provide a copy of the IEP and procedural safeguards, and check below:

☐ Did not attend (document efforts to involve parent)
☐ Via telephone
☐ Other _____

ANGELICA MALIUANAG

Angelica Maliuanag is a 20-year-old Filipino American young adult who is educationally classi-fied as having an intellectual disability.

Family and Cultural Background

Angelica lives at home with her mother, father, and one younger sister. Angelica has an older brother attending the state university and an older sister who is married and has two children. Mr. Maliuanag works full-time as an engineer, and Mrs. Maliuanag works part-time as a pediatric nurse. Having emigrated from the Philippines to the United States as children, both of Angelica's parents speak English and Tagalog fluently. Angelica speaks only English and understands some Tagalog. Her parents have asked the school to provide services to Angelica solely in English.

The Maliuanags have been very appreciative of the education provided to Angelica and have shown their respect to school personnel by accepting all of their educational recommendations. They are not concerned about Angelica achieving independence because they feel familial obligation, devotion, and loyalty to taking care of a more needy and dependent member of their family. They are concerned, however, about Angelica turning 22 years old and no longer being eligible for special education services. They want Angelica to have job training at the Flower Farm and Garden, a local nursery owned and operated by Mrs. Maliuanag's brother-in-law. They feel confident that this would provide life-long employment for Angelica in a family business with employers and employees who will care about the special needs and circumstances of their daughter.

Prior School Experience

Angelica's parents became concerned that she was delayed in meeting major developmental milestones when she was a year old. When Angelica was 18 months old, their pediatrician referred the family to the local early intervention program, where she was subsequently evalu-ated and determined eligible to receive services for toddlers with developmental delays. She received developmental, communication, and physical therapy services in the home and at the Early Intervention Center. When she turned 3 years old, she attended a preschool that enrolled half of the students who had developmental delays and half who did not have delays. At age 5, Angelica began kindergarten at her neighborhood school.

Throughout her elementary school years, she was educated alongside her nondisabled peers and was provided in-class support by special educators, para-educators, and related service pro-fessionals, in accordance with her IEP. In junior high school, Angelica began receiving some spe-cial education services in a classroom for students with disabilities, and in high school she began taking classes in the transition program, where she engaged in career exploration and learned essential work habits.

Current Schooling

After completion of her senior year, Angelica enrolled in the school district postsecondary vocational program for students with intellectual disabilities: the college-to-career program, coordinated by Mr. Budo. The curriculum in this program is individualized according to each student's IEP and provides opportunities for students to take classes with their same-age peers at the college, complete apprenticeships, participate in social and recreational activities, and hold jobs on campus or in the community. The college-to-career program is housed at the local community college and is attended by 30 students age 18–21. Of these students, 12 (40%) are white, 7 (23%) are Hispanic, 5 (17%) are Asian, 4 (13%) are African American, and 2 (7%) are from other ethnic/racial categories. Also, 5 (17%) have limited English proficiency.

At the community college, Angelica is enrolled in a modern dance class and a floral design class, and is a volunteer at the media center, where she sorts and stacks media materials. She is enrolled in math, reading, daily life skills, and employability classes with other students who have disabilities. She works alongside nondisabled peers for 2 hours a day on the grounds crew and is paid a competitive wage. Another grounds crew member is her job coach, supported by funds from Vocational Rehabilitation. Angelica especially enjoys her floral design course and her employment maintaining the grounds of the campus. Mrs. Maliuanag's brother-in-law has agreed to let Angelica work at the Flower Farm and Garden and to provide her with training and a competitive wage.

INDIVIDUALIZED EDUCATION PROGRAM

Student: _Angelica Maliuanag_   Birth date: _5/15/_   IEP date: _5/20/_

School: _College-to-Career Center_   Grade: _12+_   Classification: _Intellectual Disability_

Present Levels of Academic Achievement and Functional Performance

Preschool students: Describe how the disability affects the student's participation in appropriate activities.

School-age students: Describe how the disability affects the student's involvement and progress in the general curriculum.

MATH: Informal assessment (April 6) indicates that Angelica can use a calculator to compute addition and subtraction problems, but she cannot compute to four digits with more than 65% accuracy or compute two-digit multiplication and division problems with more than 50% accuracy. When asked, Angelica can give the names and values of coins, but she cannot count pennies beyond 20 cents or use the "dollar more" strategy to values beyond $10. She can use a debit card when purchasing items, but she cannot use it independently with more than 25% accuracy. She can read time on a digital clock, but she cannot follow her daily schedule with more than 50% accuracy. Angelica needs to use the commutative, associative, and distributive properties to add, subtract, and multiply whole numbers (EE.N-CN.2.a; alternate curriculum); count coins to $1.00 and currency to $25; use her debit card with at least 75% accuracy; and tell time to follow her daily schedule with at least 80% accuracy.

LANGUAGE ARTS: Based on informal passage fluency measures (April 3), Angelica has mastered English reading standards to a 3.5-grade level, reading 40 words correct per minute, but she cannot use accuracy, fluency, or comprehension skills to read books of her choice because they are typically written at a 5.5-grade level or higher. Based on classroom observations and skill checklists (March and April), Angelica can upload pictures from her smart phone, but she cannot write posts independently with more than 50% accuracy. She has mastered writing composition to the 2.0-grade level, but she cannot use a spell checker with more than 50% accuracy to check her work (she has difficulty choosing the right spelling for each word she is checking). Angelica needs to read text comprised of familiar words with accuracy and understanding at the 5.0-grade level and use context to confirm or self-correct word recognition when reading (EE.RF.5.4), and write to share information supported by details and with correct spelling (EE.W.5.2).

SOCIAL/EMOTIONAL: Angelica is quiet and reticent, but she has two best friends who encourage her to engage in activities that are out of her comfort zone, such as taking a modern dance class. Angelica can make choices on her own approximately 10% of the time, but she currently cannot make choices without being presented with two options (in picture form) and with verbal prompting. Angelica can set goals for her learning, but she currently cannot set goals without verbal and pictorial prompting. She can monitor her task performance, but she currently cannot do so without step-by-step verbal and pictorial prompting. To prepare for independent living, Angelica needs to make choices, set learning goals, and monitor her performance with greater levels of independence.

COMMUNICATION: Angelica can speak English and understands some Tagalog; however, she cannot initiate conversations with anyone besides her family and closest friends. Angelica can articulate clearly, but she cannot use more than simple one- to five-word phrases more than 10% of the time. She can talk about her favorite singer and TV show, but currently she cannot initiate conversation on other topics. To participate more fully in social relationships, Angelica needs to initiate and sustain conversation with more individuals on a wider range of topics.

FUNCTIONAL LIFE SKILLS: Angelica can use the city light rail system to get from her house to the community college, but she currently cannot independently take the rail to other places that are important to her, such as her friends' houses and the Flower Farm and Garden. She can shop at the grocery store with personal assistance and can make five simple cold meals using a picture-based cookbook and video modeling. Her mother has added hot meal recipes and accompanying pictures to Angelica's recipe book, but Angelica cannot yet make hot meals. To prepare for independent living, Angelica needs to increase her independence with accessing the rail system, shopping, and preparing meals.

CAREER/VOCATIONAL: Angelica participated in a job sampling program when she was in high school and found that she enjoys working in environments that are quiet and where the social and communication demands are not high. In her current work on the grounds crew, Angelica can engage in most gardening maintenance tasks (e.g., picking up litter, replacing and posting signs, weeding, cultivating), but she currently cannot complete these tasks without verbal prompting. She has not yet participated in the other tasks available to the grounds crew: plant and floral; site development; and recycling of flowers, plants, food waste, and old building materials. To prepare her for a wider range of vocational opportunities, Angelica needs to engage independently in a wider range of work tasks.

Measurable Annual Goals

1. **MATH:** *When assessed at the end of the school year, Angelica will increase her math skills to at least 80% accuracy in each of the following skill areas: four-digit addition and subtraction problems using a calculator, two-digit multiplication and division problems using a calculator, count coins to values of $1.00, use a debit card for making purchases, and read time on a digital clock to follow her daily schedule.*

Benchmarks/Short-Term Objectives

a. *When given a functional math problem requiring four-digit addition and subtraction or two-digit multiplication and division, Angelica will use a calculator to find the sum/difference/product/quotient, with at least 80% accuracy, using two different types of calculators (e.g., standard calculator, phone calculator application), and maintain the skill when probed weekly for at least 4 weeks.*

b. *When given a stack of coins adding up to no more than $1.00, Angelica will count the coins with at least 80% accuracy over 10 consecutive trials, using various coin combinations, and will maintain this skill when probed weekly for at least 4 weeks.*

c. *When Angelica is purchasing an item from a store, she will use her debit card with at least four of the six task components completed independently, in at least two different settings, and maintain this skill when probed monthly for at least 4 weeks.*

d. *When her phone alert indicates it is time to switch an activity (e.g., catch the bus, clock in at work, go to class), Angelica will independently read the time on her phone to follow her schedule with at least 80% accuracy over one week, in at least three different settings, and maintain this skill when probed weekly for at least 4 weeks.*

Student's progress toward goal measured by:

☐ formal assessment ☐ criterion-referenced test ☒ curriculum-based assessment
☐ checklists ☐ work samples ☐ self-monitoring

2. **LANGUAGE ARTS:** *When assessed at the end of the school year, Angelica will choose and read 4.0-grade level books in English with at least 52 words correct per minute and answer literal comprehension questions with at least 80% accuracy. When given access to social media sites, Angelica will upload pictures and write posts independently using a spell checker with at least 80% accuracy over 2 consecutive weeks, using at least two different sites, and maintain this skill when probed weekly for at least 4 weeks.*

Benchmarks/Short-Term Objectives

a. *When given a choice of books written in English on a 4.0-grade level, Angelica will choose a book and independently read it with at least 52 words correct per minute, with at least three books on different topics, and maintain this skill when probed weekly for at least 4 weeks.*

b. *When given a choice of books written in English on a 4.0-grade level, Angelica will choose and independently read a book, and answer end-of-chapter literal comprehension questions with at least 80% accuracy, with at least three books on different topics, and maintain this skill when probed weekly for at least 4 weeks.*

c. *When given access to social media sites, Angelica will upload pictures and write posts independently with at least 80% accuracy over 2 consecutive weeks, using at least two different sites, and maintain this skill when probed weekly for at least 4 weeks.*

d. *When given access to social media sites, Angelica will upload pictures and write posts independently using a spell checker with at least 80% accuracy over 2 consecutive weeks, using at least two different sites, and maintain this skill when probed weekly for at least 4 weeks.*

Student's progress toward goal measured by:
☐ formal assessment   ☐ criterion-referenced test   ☐ curriculum-based assessment
☒ checklists   ☐ work samples   ☐ self-monitoring

3. **SOCIAL/EMOTIONAL:** *When presented with at least two choices of activities, Angelica will make choices independently at least 60% of the time. When given picture prompts of chosen activities, Angelica will set goals independently for achievement related to these activities and self-monitor her performance on a teacher-made checklist with at least 50% accuracy.*

Benchmarks/Short-Term Objectives

a. *When presented with pictures and verbal cues of at least two choices of activities, Angelica will make choices independently at least 60% of the time over 4 consecutive school days, and maintain this skill when probed weekly for at least 4 weeks with at least four different types of activities.*

b. *When given picture prompts of chosen activities, Angelica will set goals independently for achievement related to these activities, with at least 50% accuracy, and maintain this skill when probed weekly for at least 4 weeks with at least four different activities.*

c. *When given picture prompts of chosen activities, Angelica will set goals independently for achievement related to these activities and self-monitor her performance on a teacher-made checklist, with at least 50% accuracy, and maintain this skill when probed weekly for at least 4 weeks with at least four different activities.*

Student's progress toward goal measured by:
☐ formal assessment   ☐ criterion-referenced test   ☐ curriculum-based assessment
☒ checklists   ☐ work samples   ☐ self-monitoring

4. **COMMUNICATION:** *When in a social setting with peers, Angelica will initiate conversation and discuss a range of at least five different topics with at least five-word sentences and/or phrases over at least 50% of observed occurrences, and maintain this skill when probed weekly for at least 4 weeks.*

Benchmarks/Short-Term Objectives

a. *When with a new friend or an acquaintance and using a picture prompt, Angelica will initiate conversation in at least 50% of observed occurrences and maintain this skill when probed weekly for at least 4 weeks.*

b. *When with a new friend or an acquaintance and using a picture prompt, Angelica will discuss a new topic in at least 50% of observed occurrences and maintain this skill when probed weekly for at least 4 weeks, on at least five different topics.*

c. *When with a new friend or an acquaintance and using a picture prompt, Angelica will discuss a topic using at least five-word sentences and/or phrases at least 50% of observed occurrences and maintain this skill when probed weekly for at least 4 weeks, on at least five different topics.*

Student's progress toward goal measured by:

☐ formal assessment   ☐ criterion-referenced test   ☐ curriculum-based assessment
☒ checklists   ☐ work samples   ☐ self-monitoring

5. **FUNCTIONAL LIFE SKILLS:** *When tested at the end of the school year and given pictorial and/or video support, Angelica will independently use the city bus system, shop at the grocery store, and prepare simple hot and cold meals with at least 80% accuracy.*

Benchmarks/Short-Term Objectives

a. *When scheduled to go to a location in town (e.g., Flower Farm and Garden, friend's house) and after watching a video model, Angelica will use the light rail accurately to arrive safely and on time, with 100% accuracy and with no personal assistant, and maintain this skill when probed weekly for at least 2 months.*

b. *When given a visual support system (written and picture-based cues), Angelica will purchase grocery items needed to make a meal, with at least 80% accuracy over 3 days, and maintain this skill when probed weekly for at least 2 months.*

c. *After watching a video model, and when given a picture-based cookbook, Angelica will select and make a hot or cold meal independently, with at least 80% accuracy, and maintain this skill with at least five hot and 10 cold meals when probed weekly for at least 2 months.*

Student's progress toward goal measured by:

☐ formal assessment   ☐ criterion-referenced test   ☐ curriculum-based assessment
☒ checklists   ☐ work samples   ☐ self-monitoring

6. **CAREER/VOCATIONAL:** *When working on the grounds crew and given picture prompts, Angelica will complete independently a range of at least five various tasks (e.g., picking up litter, replacing and posting signs, weeding, cultivating, recycling) with at least 80% accuracy over 3 consecutive work days, and maintain these skills when probed weekly for at least 4 weeks.*

Benchmarks/Short-Term Objectives

a. *When given one work task to complete (e.g., picking up litter, replacing and posting signs, weeding, cultivating) and picture prompts showing each step in the task, Angelica will complete the task independently, with at least 80% accuracy, over 3 consecutive work days, and maintain this skill when probed weekly for at least 4 weeks.*

b. *When given one new work task to complete (e.g., plant and floral; site development; recycling of flowers, plants, food waste, and old building materials), and picture prompts showing each step in the task, Angelica will complete the task independently, with at least 80% accuracy, over 3 consecutive work days, and maintain this skill when probed weekly for at least 4 weeks.*

Student's progress toward goal measured by:

☐ formal assessment   ☐ criterion-referenced test   ☐ curriculum-based assessment
☒ checklists   ☒ work samples   ☐ self-monitoring

Special Education Services to Achieve Annual Goals and Advance in General Curriculum

Service	Location	Time	Frequency	Begin Date	Duration
Specially designed instruction	Regular Class Special Class **Other:** **College-to-career site**	20 hrs	Daily **Weekly** Monthly	5/21	**1 year** Other:
Specially designed instruction	Regular Class Special Class **Other:** **Job site**	14 hrs	Daily **Weekly** Monthly	5/21	**1 year** Other:

Related Services to Benefit from Special Education

Service	Location	Time	Frequency	Begin Date	Duration
Speech-language services	Regular Class Special Class **Other:** **College-to-career site**	60 min	Daily **Weekly** Monthly	5/21	**1 year** Other:

Program Modifications and/or Supplementary Aids and Services in Regular Classes

Modifications/ Personnel Support	Frequency	Supplementary Aids and Services	Frequency
Training for job coach	Daily Weekly **Monthly**	Visual support systems	**Daily** Weekly Monthly

Applicable Special Factors

Factor	Not Needed	In IEP
Positive behavior instruction and support when behavior impedes learning of student or others	✓	
Language needs for student with limited English proficiency	✓	
Braille instruction for student who is blind or visually impaired	✓	
Communication and/or language services for student who is deaf, is hard of hearing, or has other communication needs		✓
Assistive technology devices or services		✓

Participation in Regular Class, Extracurricular, and Nonacademic Activities

The student will participate in the regular class and in extracurricular and other nonacademic activities except as noted in special education and related services or listed here:

Angelica is a post–high school student and will participate in elective classes and at her worksite with her nondisabled peers at the community college except when she is receiving small-group or individualized services (e.g., speech therapy).

Schedule for Written IEP Progress Reports to Parents

	Weekly	Biweekly	Monthly	Quarterly	Semiannually
Home note	✓				
Progress report		✓			
Parent conference					✓
Report card				✓	
Other					

Transition Plan

Complete and attach for students age 16 and older.
See attached.

Participation in State and District Assessments

Participation Codes

S	Standard administration	No accommodations or modifications
A	Participate with accommodations	Does not invalidate, alter, or lower standard
M	Participate with modifications	Invalidates, alters, or lowers standard
AA	Participate using alternate assessment: ☐ Out-of-level criterion-referenced test (CRT) ☒ State alternate assessment	Aligned more closely with alternate curriculum than general education curriculum

State and District Assessment Matrix

Enter appropriate participation code for each applicable assessment.

		Criterion Referenced Tests (CRTs)				State High School Competency Test		
	Accommodations	Language Arts	Math	Science	Direct Writing Assessment	Reading	Writing	Math
Presentation	1. Directions read aloud in English							
	2. Questions read aloud in English					No		
	3. Directions signed							
	4. Questions signed					No		

		Criterion Referenced Tests (CRTs)				State High School Competency Test		
	Accommodations	Language Arts	Math	Science	Direct Writing Assessment	Reading	Writing	Math
Presentation	5. Screen reader					No		
	6. Directions—oral translation							
	7. Questions—oral translation	No			No	No	No	
	8. Large print							
	9. Magnification devices							
	10. Braille							
	11. Tactile graphics							
	12. Audio amplification devices							
	13. Visual cues							
	14. Talking materials							
	15. Bilingual word lists	—	—	—	—			
	16. Translated formulas	—		—	—	—	—	
Response	17. Word processor—no spell check		—	—				—
	18. Calculation devices	—			—	—	—	
	19. Write in test booklet							
	20. Scribe							
	21. Visual organizers							
	22. Graphic organizers							
	23. Speech-to-text conversion							
	24. Brailler							
	25. Recording device							
Setting	26. Reduce distractions to student							
	27. Reduce distractions to others							
	28. Physical access							
Timing	29. Extended time							
	30. Multiple breaks							
	31. Schedule change							
Other	32. Other: Temporary (504 only)							

No: Accommodations not allowed

—: Not applicable

Accommodations and Modifications

List specific accommodations and modifications for assessments.
Not applicable.

Alternate Assessment

State why student cannot participate in regular assessment.
Regular assessment is not required for Angelica's nondisabled peers (age 20); therefore, she will not participate in state or districtwide assessments.

State why selected alternate assessment is appropriate.
Curriculum-based and community-based alternate assessments will be used to derive appropriate instructional goals for Angelica.

Extended School Year

Extended school year (ESY) services are provided when the team determines the student will not benefit if services are not provided during the normal summer break.

☐ Student is eligible for ESY.
☒ Student is not eligible for ESY.

Placement Review

☐ Initial placement ☒ Continue placement ☐ Change placement

IEP Team Participants

Nicole Maliuanag	Parent
Joshua Maliuanag	Parent
TONY JEX	LEA representative
Angelica Maliuanag	Student
Jackson Budo	College-to-career director
Esther Williams	Speech-language pathologist
Bryan Atangan	Flower Farm and Garden
Carlos Mielke	Vocational Rehabilitation

If parent signature is missing, provide a copy of the IEP and procedural safeguards and check below:
☐ Did not attend (document efforts to involve parent)
☐ Via telephone
☐ Other _____

TRANSITION PLAN

Student: _Angelica Maliuanag_   Birth date: _5/15/_   IEP date: _5/20/_

School: _College-to-Career Center_   Grade: _12+_   Classification: _Intellectual Disability_

Transition Goals, Activities, and Services

Write the transition activities and services needed to achieve postsecondary goals. Refer to IEP goals or explain how transition activities and services will be provided. Indicate who is responsible and why services may not be needed.

1. Functional Vocational Evaluation

Services Needed to Achieve Goals	Agency Responsible
Administer functional vocational evaluation	Vocational Rehabilitation

OR indicate why service is not needed:
☐ Student functions independently in work settings.
☒ Other: _While Angelica currently works on the grounds crew with a job coach, she would like to begin working at the Flower Farm and Garden. An evaluation of the demands of this job and Angelica's skills will need to be conducted._

2. Education. See IEP goal(s) ___1–4___, or indicate here:
☐ Graduate with a regular diploma   ☒ Postsecondary education
☒ Graduate with a certificate of completion   ☐ Other: _____

Services Needed to Achieve Goals	Agency Responsible
College-to-career program	School district, partnering with community college
Specialized instruction	School district
Speech-language services	School district

3. Training. See IEP goal(s) ___6___, or indicate here:

Services Needed to Achieve Goals	Agency Responsible
Job coach	School district

OR indicate why service is not needed:
☐ Student functions independently in work settings.
☐ Other: _____

4. Employment. See IEP goal(s) ___6___, or list here:

Services Needed to Achieve Goals	Agency Responsible
On-the-job training	School district, in partnership with college

OR indicate why service is not needed:
☐ Student functions independently in work settings.
☐ Other: _____

5. Independent Living. See IEP goal(s) ___5___, or indicate here:

Housing
- ☐ Skilled care facility
- ☐ Group home
- ☐ Supervised apartment
- ☐ Supported living
- ☒ Family home
- ☐ Apartment
- ☐ Home of own
- ☐ Other: _____

Transportation
- ☐ Independent transportation (e.g., walk, bicycle, car)
- ☒ Public transportation (e.g., bus, train)
- ☐ Specialized transportation
- ☐ Other: _____

Services Needed to Achieve Goals	Agency Responsible
Bus pass	*School district*

OR indicate why service is not needed:
- ☐ Student functions independently.
- ☐ Other: _____

6. Daily Living Skills, if appropriate. See IEP goal(s) ___5___, or list here:

Services Needed to Achieve Goals	Agency Responsible
Special education	*School district*

OR indicate why service is not needed:
- ☐ Student functions independently in work settings.
- ☐ Other: _____

Age of Majority

On or before the student's 17th birthday, inform the student and parent(s) of transfer of rights at age 18.
Date informed: _April 2_ _____

Nonparticipation in Transition Planning

If the student did not participate in this plan, indicate the steps taken to ensure that the student's preferences were considered.

Not applicable. Angelica participated in developing this plan.

If a representative of an agency responsible for providing an activity did not participate, indicate the steps that will be taken to obtain the participation of the agency.

Not applicable. Representatives from Vocational Rehabilitation, College-to-Career, and Flower Farm and Garden participated in developing this plan.

Describe the Student's Present Levels of Academic Achievement and Functional Performance

The Individuals with Disabilities Education Improvement Act (IDEA) requires that the individualized education program (IEP) include a statement of the student's present levels of academic achievement and functional performance (PLAAFP). Stating a student's PLAAFP is the first step in the IEP process because this information is the basis for selecting reasonable goals for the year's improvement.

What is a PLAAFP statement?

A PLAAFP statement is a brief but detailed description of a student's achievement and functional performance at the time the IEP is created. This description is derived from formal and informal assessments conducted by the team, from the student's level of progress on the previous IEP goals, and from consideration of the student's grade-level curriculum standards. The PLAAFP statement must address all areas affected by the disability. For example, because Ricky's emotional disturbance affects his school behavior and his progress in the general curriculum, his PLAAFP statement addresses both functional behavior and academic achievement. Let's take a look at the terms *academic achievement* and *functional performance*.

Academic achievement refers to gaining requisite skills and knowledge for success in school. The most important academic skills students learn are reading, writing, and math because these skills are foundational for achievement in other academic areas such as science, health, and social studies.

Functional performance can be defined as applying knowledge and skills to meet daily needs. Included are social skills such as engaging in healthy relationships and meeting school behavior expectations, as well as adaptive skills such as feeding and dressing oneself, participating in recreational activities, shopping for groceries, and applying and interviewing for a job.

Why differentiate between academic achievement and functional performance?

Academic achievement and functional performance are differentiated for students depending on their age and on the effects of disabilities on their learning. Most students' education will focus primarily on the general curriculum, so their PLAAFP statements will center on academic achievement. Other students will need to gain functional living skills along with academic skills; therefore, their PLAAFP statements will describe both functional performance and academic needs.

Generally the larger the gap between a student's academic or functional performance and age-appropriate core curriculum, the more likely the student's IEP will address functional skills. For example, a 5-year-old child who does not correctly identify colors may have an academic goal for obtaining this skill. However, an 18-year-old student who does not correctly identify colors might have a more functional goal to prepare for adult living, such as sorting dark and light colors for laundry.

Why are PLAAFP statements important?

PLAAFP statements provide a starting point for all decisions regarding a student's individualized education. Teachers must understand what students know and can do before planning the next steps. For example, if a teacher asks a student to read from *The Cat in the Hat* by Dr. Seuss, but the student is unable to decode simple words, the result will be frustration and failure. Knowing the student's reading skill level guides the teacher toward an appropriate starting point.

THE MORE ACCURATELY THE TEAM CAN DESCRIBE PRESENT LEVELS OF ACADEMIC ACHIEVEMENT AND FUNCTIONAL PERFORMANCE, THE MORE LIKELY THEY ARE TO PLAN APPROPRIATE ANNUAL GOALS FOR IMPROVEMENT.

How does my team obtain information for developing a PLAAFP statement?

Obtaining the necessary information requires three steps: review the curriculum standards for academic achievement, determine the student's current academic strengths and limitations, and assess the student's current functional strengths and limitations. We describe these below.

1. **Review the curriculum standards for academic achievement.**
   Access your state's curriculum standards, and review the requirements for the student's grade level. Because an IEP must provide goals and attendant services required to help the student engage and progress in the general curriculum, the team should use the grade-level curriculum standards as guideposts to determine the student's goals for improvement. For example, the math Common Core standard for numbers and operations in base 10 states that a third-grade student should "use place value understanding to round whole numbers to the nearest 10 or 100" (CCSS. Math.Content.3.NBT.A.1). This standard will serve as a later example for crafting a PLAAFP statement.

   STANDARDS-BASED IEPs

   The term *standards-based IEP* refers to PLAAFP statements and associated annual goals developed according to a state's academic curriculum standards. States can either create their own grade-level standards for academic subjects or adopt the Common Core State Standards (National Governors Association Center for Best Practices, Council of Chief State School Officers, 2010).

2. **Determine the student's current *academic* strengths and limitations.**
   Multidisciplinary teams use both formal and informal assessment to determine student academic achievement. Formal assessment is typically used to determine eligibility for special education; informal assessment is used to guide daily instruction.

Formal Assessment

Formal assessments are standardized tests, meaning that the assessor follows a prescribed administration protocol for each student, or they are norm-referenced tests, which compare student achievement to a similar population based on age or grade level, or both. Formal assessments include tests of intelligence and tests of academic achievement. Intelligence tests broadly measure cognitive aptitude, indicating a student's ability to process information as required for learning, and yield an IQ score.

Common standardized cognitive tests include the *Wechsler Intelligence Scale for Children*, the *Stanford-Binet Intelligence Scales,* and others. Common tests of achievement include the *Woodcock-Johnson Psychoeducational Battery,* the *Wechsler Individual Achievement Test,* the *Kaufman Test of Educational Achievement,* and others. Standardized tests of specific skill areas include *Key Math*, *Woodcock Diagnostic Reading Battery,* and others.

Informal Assessment

Informal assessment may include criterion-referenced tests, curriculum-based assessments and measures, and teacher or parent checklists. Criterion-referenced tests compare student achievement to set criteria, such as the *Brigance Comprehensive Inventory of Basic Skills*, *Dynamic Indicators of Basic Early Literacy Skills* (DIBELS), some core curriculum tests designed by state offices of education, and alternate assessments designed for students with significant cognitive disabilities. Curriculum-based assessments measure student performance directly from the current curriculum, such as placement tests for a math program, and curriculum-based measures, such as teacher-made tests to check systematically progress toward mastering math facts.

Classroom teachers can provide observational anecdotes, skills checklists, and student work samples to help the team understand a student's strengths and needs. Teachers are also good sources of information about student behavior and interpersonal relations with other students.

Parents or other caregivers are valuable sources of information. They know the student better than the school does and can give insight into interests, hobbies, and talents. Parents can complete behavioral or functional living checklists, and they can also enlighten the team regarding a student's history of success or failure and strategies that have worked well in the past.

Returning to our third-grade Common Core math example, a team member can use data from a recent formal test or from an informal test with several sample problems to measure a student's ability to use place value understanding to round whole numbers to the nearest 10 or 100. If results show that the student can round to the nearest 10 but not to the nearest 100, then the team will note this performance gap in the PLAAFP statement.

3. **Assess the student's current *functional* strengths and limitations.**
   Similar to determining a student's academic performance, the team uses formal and informal assessment along with parent input to identify a student's functional strengths and

limitations. Formal assessments of adaptive functioning include norm-referenced tests such as the *Vineland Adaptive Behavior Scales, Scales of Independent Behavior,* and the *Adaptive Behavior Scale*. Other formal assessments measure students' prosocial or maladaptive behavior, such as the *Behavior Observation Sequence* and the *Behavior Assessment System for Children*. These assessments are usually completed by classroom teachers, school psychologists, and/or parents.

Informal assessment involves criterion-referenced tests that compare students' functional skills to set criteria, such as the *Brigance Diagnostic Inventory of Early Development, Checklist of Adaptive Living Skills,* and state or district alternate assessments designed for students with significant cognitive disabilities.

TEACHING FUNCTIONAL SKILLS

> It is important to teach functional skills in an environment as close as possible to that in which they will be used. For example, if a parent wants her son to learn to make his bed and the school has no bed for practice, the student is not likely to generalize instruction in bed making from school to home; this skill is better taught in the natural home environment.

Collaboration with parents is critical when assessing functional skills. Skills that are functional at school may not be functional at home, and vice versa, so school professionals and parents must work closely together to describe students' present levels of functional performance across environments.

The team summarizes relevant data from these various sources to describe the student's present levels of academic achievement and functional performance in areas affected by the student's disability. These data are useful for determining the gap between the student's current achievement and relevant standards.

How does my team create a PLAAFP statement?

IDEA requires your team to do the following when creating a PLAAFP statement:

1. Describe how the disability affects the student's academic achievement and functional performance in the relevant skill areas.

2. For elementary or secondary students, describe how the disability affects the student's involvement and progress in the general education curriculum.

3. For preschool students, describe how the disability affects the student's participation in appropriate activities.

In practice, teams often include a statement of the student's strengths as well as the effects of the disability on the individual's achievement or functional performance. This strengths-based approach more accurately portrays the student's functioning by stating what he or she has mastered within the curriculum. The common format for this type of PLAAFP statement has three parts, focused in reference to relevant standards:

1. A description of the student's academic or functional strengths, sometimes referred to as "can do."

2. A description of the student's academic or functional limitations, or "cannot do."

3. A statement of needed improvement to progress in the general curriculum, or "needs to."

A well-written PLAAFP has sufficient detail to provide descriptive and logical cues for writing the accompanying annual goals.

What if the demands of the general curriculum are too high for some students?

IDEA recognizes that a few students' disabilities are likely to prevent them from meeting grade-level standards in the general curriculum, even with appropriate accommodations and modifications (34 CFR §300.320[a][2][ii]). All students are required to take state assessments to meet accountability standards of the No Child Left Behind (NCLB) Act. However, NCLB states that up to 2% of a state's or district's students (approximately 20% of students with disabilities) may take alternate assessments aligned to alternate achievement standards (34 CFR §200.13[c][2][ii]). IEP teams decide which students will take standard assessments, with or without modifications or accommodations, and which students will take alternate assessments. You will learn more about this in Step 6.

Alternate achievement standards, sometimes referred to as *extended standards*, are created and adopted by individual states. NCLB requires states to link alternate standards to the grade-level core standards; they may be reduced in breadth or depth, but they must be appropriately challenging. For example, Dynamic Learning Maps Essential Elements (EE) (University of Kansas, 2010) alternate standards indicate that, where the first-grade Common Core requires students to decode regularly spelled one-syllable words (RF.1.3), students with significant cognitive disabilities will, with guidance and support, recognize familiar words that are used in everyday routines (EE.RF.1.3; Utah State Office of Education, n.d.). Alternate achievement standards are the reference for developing academic PLAAFP statements for these students.

What does a PLAAFP statement look like?

Here is the PLAAFP statement for reading from eighth-grade student Jameelah's IEP:

> *Informal passage fluency measures (1/21/__) show Jameelah has mastered oral reading standards to the fifth-grade level but cannot read sixth- or seventh-grade passages fluently. Woodcock-Johnson Tests of Achievement (1/28/__) indicate she has mastered passage comprehension standards to fifth-grade level, but she cannot comprehend accurately at the sixth-grade level or beyond. To progress in the eighth-grade general curriculum, Jameelah needs to read and comprehend literature, including stories, dramas, and poems, at the high end of the grades 6 to 8 text complexity band independently and proficiently (CCSS.ELA-LITERACY.RI.8.10).*

Does Jameelah's PLAAFP include the necessary elements?

Yes it does, but let's take a closer look at the statement to see *how* it includes the necessary elements:

1. It describes how the disability affects the student's academic achievement and functional performance in the relevant skill areas.

    > *Jameelah has mastered oral reading standards to the fifth-grade level but cannot read sixth- or seventh-grade passages fluently. Woodcock-Johnson Tests of Achievement (1/28/___) indicate she has mastered passage comprehension standards to the fifth-grade level, but she cannot comprehend accurately at sixth-grade level or beyond.*

2. It states how the disability affects the student's engagement and progress in the general education curriculum.

> *To progress in the eighth-grade general curriculum, Jameelah needs to read and comprehend literature, including stories, dramas, and poems, at the high end of the grades 6 to 8 text complexity band independently and proficiently (CCSS.ELA-LITERACY.RI.8.10).*

3. If this IEP were for a preschool student, it would state, as appropriate, how the disability affects the student's participation in appropriate activities.

> This does not apply to Jameelah because she is in the eighth grade. If she were a preschool student, it might state that she is able to participate in parallel play with other children but is not ready for contexts requiring student interaction.

May I see another example?

Sure. Here is the math PLAAFP statement from Angelica's IEP, which does not reference the Common Core curriculum because she is beyond high school age and is one of the few students whose significant cognitive disabilities are best addressed with an alternate curriculum:

MATH: Informal assessment (April 6) indicates that Angelica can use a calculator to compute addition and subtraction problems, but she cannot compute to four digits with more than 65% accuracy or compute two-digit multiplication and division problems with more than 50% accuracy. When asked, Angelica can give the names and values of coins, but she cannot count pennies beyond 20 cents or use the "dollar more" strategy to values beyond $10. She can use a debit card when purchasing items, but she cannot use it independently with more than 25% accuracy. She can read time on a digital clock, but she cannot follow her daily schedule with more than 50% accuracy. Angelica needs to use the commutative, associative, and distributive properties to add, subtract, and multiply whole numbers (EE.N-CN.2.a; alternate curriculum); count coins to $1.00 and currency to $25; use her debit card with 75% accuracy; and tell time to follow her daily schedule with at least 80% accuracy.

Does Angelica's example include the necessary elements?

Yes it does, but let's look closely at the statement so you can see *how* it includes the necessary elements for a student with significant cognitive disabilities whose needs fall within an alternate academic curriculum:

1. It describes how the disability affects the student's academic achievement and functional performance in the relevant skill areas.

> *Angelica can use a calculator to compute addition and subtraction problems, but she cannot compute to four digits with more than 65% accuracy or compute two-digit multiplication and division problems with more than 50% accuracy. When asked, Angelica can give the names and values of coins, but she cannot count pennies beyond 20 cents or use the "dollar more" strategy to values beyond $10. She can use a debit card when purchasing items, but she cannot use it independently with more than 25% accuracy. She can read time on a digital clock, but she cannot follow her daily schedule with more than 50% accuracy.*

2. It states how the disability affects the student's involvement and progress in the general education curriculum.

> *Angelica is learning an alternative curriculum suited to her functional needs rather than the general curriculum.*

3. If this IEP were for a preschool student, it would state, as appropriate, how the disability affects the student's participation in appropriate activities.

> This does not apply to Angelica since she is in the 12th grade.

What about PLAAFP statements for students with behavioral needs?

Behavioral expectations are not usually listed as hierarchical standards the way that academics are, so team members must identify and define student behaviors that are and are not appropriate and productive in various settings. Teams use observation data summarized as detailed descriptions of behavior to create appropriate PLAAFP statements. Observation formats describe behaviors, such as *in seat, out of seat, talking out, hitting,* and *noncompliance with teacher directives,* and record frequency, duration, and/or latency data.

Teams must use multiple observations over different days, times, and environments to determine if student behavior is pervasive, contextual, or just an occasional bad day. IEPs should address measurable behaviors that consistently interfere with the student's progress in the general curriculum or interfere with the learning of other students.

> HAVING A FEW BAD BEHAVIOR DAYS IS NOT THE SAME AS HAVING SERIOUS EMOTIONAL DISTURBANCE. SOMETIMES THINGS JUST DON'T GO WELL FOR STUDENTS, BUT THAT DOESN'T MEAN THEY HAVE A DISABILITY.

May I see an example?

Sure. Let's look at Ricky's PLAAFP statement, which addresses his behavior:

During three 30-minute classroom observations (9/15/__, 9/17/__, 9/23/__), Ricky refused to comply with teacher requests or directives an average of seven out of seven times and pushed reading materials away or off his desk an average of three out of three times. During two 15-minute cafeteria observations (9/16, 10/18) Ricky had two instances each of pushing students out of line, cutting in the food and tray deposit lines, and verbally refusing an adult's reminders that these behaviors are against the rules. Ricky needs to decrease behavior outbursts in the classroom and cafeteria and to increase compliance with teacher directives to interact appropriately with others to progress in the general curriculum.

Notice that Ricky's PLAAFP describes these behaviors:

- *Refused to comply with teacher requests or directives*

- *Pushed reading materials away or off his desk*

- *Pushed students out of line*

- *Cut in the food and tray deposit lines*

- *Verbally refused an adult's reminders that these behaviors are against the rules*

The IEP also includes how the behavior was measured:

- *During three 30-minute classroom observations (9/15/__, 9/17/__, 9/23/__)*

- *During two 15-minute cafeteria observations (9/16, 10/18)*

It notes the number or degree of occurrences:

- *An average of seven out of seven times*

- *An average of three out of three times*

- *Two instances each*

And it includes a "needs to" statement:

Ricky needs to decrease behavior outbursts in the classroom and cafeteria and to increase compliance with teacher directives to interact appropriately with others to progress in the general curriculum.

Now it's your turn.

Here are assessment data for Samuel, a fourth-grade student with intellectual disabilities who is learning in the general curriculum. Your task is to summarize the data into a brief but descriptive PLAAFP for Samuel's IEP. When you have finished, check your PLAAFP with our suggestion in the appendix.

Achievement Testing

- **Math Calculation:** 9/10 one-digit addition and subtraction correct; 0/10 two-digit and one-digit without renaming correct; 0/5 multiplication and division correct.

- **Written expression:** Dictates simple sentences when given a subject, 5/5 correct; writes simple sentences when given a subject, 0/5 correct.

Functional Skills Assessment

- **Self-Help Skills:** Correctly selects his backpack in a group of others but does not place school materials in the backpack without prompting. Uses the restroom independently but does not fasten pants or wash hands without reminding.

- **Socialization:** Starts, joins, and maintains a conversation with peers but does not end a conversation without prompting; interrupts others in their conversations.

PLAAFP for Samuel:

_____

_____

_____

_____

_____

Common Errors

Here are errors that are common in writing PLAAFP statements:

1. Writing a statement with vague descriptions of achievement or performance
   "Sophia is earning a C– in math."
   "Emma's reading standard score is 84."
   "Mason can't control his behaviors in public."

2. Writing a statement that is not related to the student's curriculum
   "Ava is very helpful at home."
   "Maya is a conscientious teacher assistant."
   "Noah eats his breakfast without assistance."

3. Writing a statement that is not related to the student's disability
   "Luis [with a reading disability] has excellent grades in band and chorus."
   "Yulia [5-year-old with a speech fluency disorder] knows her colors and shapes."

4. Writing a "can do" statement but no "cannot" or "does not do" statement
   "Leilani knows her letter names and sounds and can sound out simple words."

"Sangeetha behaves appropriately in a well-structured setting."

"Billi has learned to ride the bus independently."

5. For a preschooler, writing a statement that does not indicate how the disability affects the student's participation in appropriate activities

"Francesco [3 years old] is unable to state his birth date." (Most 3-year-olds cannot do this so it is not an appropriate activity.)

"Cyrus [4 years old] cannot sit for more than 30 minutes to listen to the teacher read a story." (Four-year-olds are not expected to sit and listen for 30 minutes so this is not an appropriate activity.)

"Quon [4 years old] is unable to match upper- and lowercase letters on a worksheet." (Four-year-olds generally do not use worksheets, and the task is too complex for her age, so this is not an appropriate activity.)

Now you try some.

For each incomplete or poorly written PLAAFP statement below, indicate the common errors. Check your answers with ours in the appendix.

PLAAFP statement: *"Kingston [14-year-old boy] initiates and sustains conversations with peers and can call his friends on the telephone."*

Error:_____

_____

PLAAFP statement: *"Evangeline [9-year-old girl with specific learning disabilities in reading] writes all uppercase and lowercase letters in isolation and in words. She does not form closed letters correctly. Her penmanship skills inhibit her progress in the general writing curriculum."*

Error:_____

_____

PLAAFP statement: *"McCoy [6-year-old boy] is often out of control and is unhappy with school."*

Error:_____

_____

Let's review the elements of a PLAAFP statement.

A PLAAFP statement must include these three elements:

1. A description of how the disability affects the student's academic achievement and functional performance in relevant skill areas

2. For K–12 students, a statement of how the disability affects the student's involvement and progress in the general education curriculum

3. For preschool students, an explanation of how the disability affects the student's participation in appropriate activities

In practice, the PLAAFP may include these elements and references relevant standards:

1. A description of the student's strengths, sometimes referred to as "can do"

2. A description of the student's limitations, or "cannot do"

3. A statement of needed improvement to progress in the general curriculum, or "needs to"

The statement should look like this for a student with academic needs:

Duncan [second grade] **can** say all letter names and sounds. DIBELS testing of 1/21 shows that he **cannot** read second-grade oral reading passages at the midyear benchmark of 72 words correct per minute (wcpm). He cannot answer literal or inferential reading comprehension questions from DIBELS oral reading fluency passages. He **needs to** read with sufficient accuracy and fluency to support comprehension to progress in the general curriculum. (CCSS.ELA.LITERACY.RF.2.4)

CONGRATULATIONS! YOU HAVE COMPLETED STEP 1. LET'S MOVE ON TO **STEP 2,** WRITING MEASURABLE ANNUAL GOALS.

✔ Describe the student's present levels of academic achievement and functional performance.

2 Write measurable annual goals.

3 Measure and report student progress.

4 State the services needed to achieve annual goals.

5 Explain the extent, if any, to which the student will not participate with nondisabled students in the regular class and in extracurricular and other nonacademic activities.

6 Explain accommodations necessary to measure academic achievement and functional performance on state- and districtwide assessments.

7 Complete a transition plan for students age 16 and older.

References

National Governors Association Center for Best Practices, Council of Chief State School Officers. (2010). *Common Core State Standards*. Washington, DC: Author. Retrieved from http://www.corestandards.org

University of Kansas. (2010). *Dynamic learning maps essential elements*. Lawrence, KS: Center for Educational Testing & Evaluation. Retrieved from http://dynamiclearningmaps.org/content/what-learning-map

Utah State Office of Education. (n.d.). *Dynamic learning maps. Essential elements of instruction*. Salt Lake City, UT: Author. Retrieved from http://www.schools.utah.gov/sars/Significant-Cognitive-Disabilities/Essential-Elements.aspx

2 *Write Measurable Annual Goals*

You have learned that statements of a student's present levels of academic achievement and functional performance describe how the disability affects involvement and progress in the general education curriculum. In this section, you will learn that measurable annual goals designate what the student is expected to achieve within one year to address the effects of the disability. Present levels reflect present conditions; annual goals describe future achievement.

What are measurable annual goals?

Measurable annual goals are the individualized education program (IEP) team's best estimate of what the student can accomplish in the next year. A statement of measurable academic and functional performance goals must do the following:

1. Meet the student's needs related to the disability that may interfere with his or her involvement and progress in the general education curriculum

2. Meet the student's additional educational needs resulting from the disability

3. Be measurable

What is the general education curriculum?

The general curriculum is established by a state office of education and is implemented in individual schools under the direction of school districts. Some states provide curricula consisting of a general scope and sequence for each grade level, while others use more specific measurable outcomes for each subject area in each grade. Most states participate in the Common Core State Standards Initiative, which is the reference for the sample goals in this chapter. It is important to know that students with disabilities are entitled to have access to and progress in the general curriculum like their peers without disabilities.

What are "additional educational needs resulting from the disability"?

The Individuals with Disabilities Education Improvement Act (IDEA) requires IEP teams to consider a student's academic, developmental, and functional needs. Because the designation *general education curriculum* refers mainly to academic subjects, *additional educational needs* refers to the student's developmental and functional needs that result directly from the disability. The term *developmental* refers to a predictable sequence of growth. Therefore, a student with developmental difficulties may fall considerably behind peers in areas such as self-care, language, or motor skills. *Functional* refers to applying knowledge and skills to meet everyday needs such as eating, dressing, communicating, and accessing transportation. The curriculum for a preschool child with severe disabilities may focus on developmental growth, whereas the curriculum for an adolescent with severe disabilities may focus primarily on functional living skills.

What does *measurable* mean?

The term *measurable* means the behavior stated in the goal can be observed and measured to determine when it has been achieved. For example, a goal to understand addition is not observable or measurable because it does not specify how the student will demonstrate understanding. You cannot watch a student understand; you can only see evidence of understanding in some observable form. Stated in measurable terms, the goal might be "write correct answers to addition problems" rather than "understand grade-level addition." You can observe written answers and easily measure their accuracy.

How does the IEP team set goals that are important to the student and the family?

The team sets goals that are important to the student and the family by inviting and considering their desires and opinions. You'll remember that the IEP team includes the parents or guardians, relevant school professionals, and the student when appropriate. Each team member contributes necessary perspectives toward setting appropriate goals, and parent and student perspectives are very important. Let's look at each team member's contributions.

Parents. Parents know much about what the student can reasonably accomplish, based on their child's history in the home and at school. Thus, IEP teams must consider and include parent perspectives in goal setting. Too often parents are marginalized in the goal-setting process by school personnel who are more concerned with having the student fit in with existing curricula and convenient routines than with what is actually most appropriate.

Regular classroom teacher. The regular classroom teacher understands the general curriculum and can guide the team to align IEP goals with it.

Special education teacher. The special education teacher can break down the general curriculum standards or instructional tasks in the areas affected by the student's disability in order to write reasonable goals for achievement within the year.

Related service providers. Related service providers include professionals such as speech-language pathologists, occupational therapists, physical therapists, school psychologists, and school social workers. These professionals provide assessment information in their areas of specialty to help the team develop goals for improvement in the specialty areas they represent.

Individual(s) who can interpret evaluation results. A teacher or related services provider who can explain test results should be included so that team members can understand the results and apply them in selecting appropriate goals. For example, a special education teacher can interpret achievement test results, a school psychologist can explain psychological test results, and an occupational therapist can explain the results of fine motor skill assessment.

Local education agency (LEA) representative. The LEA representative verifies the availability of resources necessary to achieve the goals. The LEA representative may be the principal, assistant principal, other school administrator, or a designee.

Other individuals with special knowledge or expertise. At the discretion of the parent or the school, participants in goal setting may include a family advocate, a cultural/linguistic interpreter, an after-school care provider, or other individual who has relevant knowledge of the disability or of the child as an individual.

Student. Student participation in goal setting helps the team understand personal likes, dislikes, and goals for the future, particularly when the IEP team begins to plan for the student's transition to adult life. Students should be invited to take part in the IEP planning when they are able to contribute.

How do I write grade-level goals when the student's achievement is well below grade level?

When the student is achieving well below grade level, the team might write goals using a bilevel approach. The bilevel approach means that one or more goals address the student's grade-level standards, and one or more goals address necessary skill improvements at a lower level. For example, for a student who cannot read at grade level, the team may consider the student's strengths that can contribute to grade-level goals without requiring reading skills the student does not have. On a lower level, subsequent goals can address the skill deficits within the same standard (Yates, 2014).

Can I see examples of bilevel annual goals?

Sure. Let's look at Jameelah, who is in eighth grade. Reading goal 1 states given stories, dramas, and poems of eighth-grade complexity read aloud to her and weekly opportunities to practice, Jameelah will say or write answers to literal and inferential questions about theme, characters, and events with at least 90% accuracy on two samples of each text type, as measured by teacher observation records and informal written work (CCSS.ELA-LITERACY.RI.8.10). The Common Core standard actually requires students to "read" and comprehend, but Jameelah cannot read eighth-grade-level material. Therefore, her first goal addresses comprehension through listening to the passages and then answering questions. This grade-level goal still addresses the comprehension requirement, but it does not rely on reading. Goals 2 and 3 require a lower level of skill because they address skill deficits for reading fluency and reading comprehension required to meet the standard.

Remember, the PLAAFP statement includes "can do," "cannot do," and "needs to" statements. The "needs to" statement identifies the grade-level standard, and the "cannot do" statements indicate skill deficits that need improvement. Therefore, begin by writing a goal for the "needs to" grade-level curriculum standard and then write goals to address the "cannot do" skill deficit(s). Let's look at the reading example from Jameelah's IEP.

PLAAFP

Informal passage fluency measures (1/21/__) show Jameelah has mastered oral reading standards to the fifth-grade level but cannot read sixth- or seventh-grade passages fluently. *Woodcock-Johnson Tests of Achievement* (1/28/__) indicate she has mastered passage comprehension standards to fifth-grade level, but she cannot comprehend accurately at the sixth-grade level or beyond. To progress in the [eighth-grade] general curriculum, Jameelah needs to read and comprehend literature, including stories, dramas, and poems, at the high end of the grades 6 to 8 text complexity band independently and proficiently (CCSS.ELA-LITERACY.RI.8.10).

Goal Indicators

Needs to. To progress in the eighth-grade general curriculum Jameelah needs to read and comprehend literature, including stories, dramas, and poems, at the high end of the grades 6 to 8 text complexity band independently and proficiently to progress in the general curriculum.

1. *Annual Goal*

   Given stories, dramas, and poems of eighth-grade complexity read aloud to her and weekly opportunities to practice, Jameelah will say or write answers to literal and inferential questions about theme, characters, and events with at least 90% or greater accuracy on two samples of each text type, as measured by teacher observation records and informal written work (CCSS.ELA-LITERACY.RI.8.10).

   Cannot do. Jameelah cannot read sixth- or seventh-grade passages fluently.

2. *Annual Goal*

   Given reading passages at seventh-grade level from fiction, nonfiction, and poetry, and weekly opportunities to practice, Jameelah will orally read each text type at 100 or more words correct per minute with at least 95% accuracy in four of five opportunities as measured by progress monitoring and teacher observation records.

   Cannot do. Jameelah cannot comprehend accurately at a sixth-grade level or beyond.

3. *Annual Goal*

   Given reading passages at the seventh-grade level from fiction, nonfiction, and poetry, and weekly opportunities to practice, Jameelah will read the passages and say or write answers to literal and inferential comprehension questions with at least 80% accuracy for four of five passages as measured by teacher observation records.

Notice the bilevel nature of the goals. The first annual goal addresses the grade-level standard, but it requires listening comprehension rather than reading comprehension. The third annual goal requires Jameelah to read and comprehend but at a more reasonable level of two grade levels above her current achievement level. Given appropriately intensive instruction and practice, it is not unreasonable for Jameelah to gain two grade levels in reading achievement.

What are the components of a measurable annual goal?

IDEA does not specify the wording for writing a measurable annual goal. The law requires only that annual goals must address progress in the general curriculum, address other needs caused by the disability, and be measurable. IEP teams usually use a format established by the school or district. In addition, best practice suggests that a truly measurable goal has at least the following four elements:

1. **The student's name.** Including the student's name personalizes the goal and ensures that anyone accessing the record knows whose needs are addressed.

2. **A description of the conditions under which the behavior will be performed.** Conditions may include instructional personnel, materials, settings, and specific instructional cues. The conditions for Jameelah's second annual goal are "given reading passages at the seventh-grade level from fiction, nonfiction, and poetry, and weekly opportunities to practice."

3. **The specific observable behavior to be performed.** This designated behavior should come from the PLAAFP statement. Observable behaviors are those the teacher can see or hear. For example, the behavior for Jameelah's third annual goal is to "orally read each text type." The teacher can hear Jameelah read but would not be able to observe how she understands, thinks, or feels about reading simply by listening. *Understands, thinks, feels,* and *knows* are not observable behaviors; therefore, these terms should not be used in writing annual goals. Similarly, the phrase *be able to* is not appropriate for the annual goal, for two reasons. First,

students may be able to engage in certain behaviors but be prevented from doing so by conditions, such as lack of access to materials, insufficient time to complete tasks, or unwillingness to complete the task (yet having the skills to do so). For example, Davida, a 10-year old girl who has an intellectual disability, can tie her own shoes. But when she is asked to do so, she often refuses. Writing a goal for her to "*be able to* tie her shoelaces" is not appropriate because she already has the skill; the skill deficit that she needs to work on is following teacher directions. Second, the wording is imprecise: The word *will* is more active and direct.

4. **The criterion to indicate the level of performance at which the goal will be achieved.** The criterion for Jameelah's third goal is "with at least 80% accuracy for four of five passages." This means that she will answer at least 80% of comprehension questions correctly from at least four of five assigned reading passages. Criteria must be related to the behavior. There are many ways to set criteria:

   - *Percentage* is appropriate where the number of trials differs from time to time, such as opportunities to engage in peer play.
   - *Number correct* or *number of allowable errors* is used when the number of trials remains constant, such as 20 spelling words each week.
   - *Rate* refers to speed and accuracy, such as the number of words read correctly in 1 minute or the number of math facts written correctly in 1 minute.
   - *Frequency* is a measure of the number of times a behavior occurs in a set time frame, such as the number of verbal outbursts in a class period.
   - *Latency* measures the time lapse between a stimulus and the desired student response. For instance, the criterion may require a student to respond to a peer's greeting within 15 seconds.
   - *Duration* indicates the length of time a behavior continues, like the number of minutes a student hits the desk before stopping.

The appropriate criterion measure for a goal is an important choice. For example, a teacher once collected frequency data on student screaming that showed that the student cried only twice per day: once from 8:00 a.m. until lunchtime, and once more from lunch until 3:00 p.m. The teacher quickly realized that duration data were more appropriate.

Consider adding two components to the annual goal.

1. **A statement of generalization indicating additional conditions under which the behavior will be performed to criterion.** Generalization criteria ensure that the student can perform the task under various circumstances, including:

   - with different people
   - in various environments
   - with varied instructional cues
   - at different times of the day
   - with different materials

For example, one of Angelica's math benchmarks requires her to follow her schedule "in at least three different settings." This is important because some students learn to perform tasks in one area, such as following a school schedule, but struggle to carry over their skills to different situations, such as following work and home schedules.

2. **A statement of maintenance indicating the student will perform the task to criterion for a specified period of time.** This is appropriate when the skill needs to be performed accurately over a period of time in order to ensure mastery. For example, a student may count to ten accurately on Friday, but be unable to do so on Monday. The student may need more opportunities to practice the skill with high levels of accuracy to ensure retention. Maintenance data do not need to be collected daily once the student has reached mastery criterion. Teachers may measure maintenance by probing, or collecting data, on a weekly or monthly basis. For example, the maintenance statement for one of Angelica's math bench-marks requires her to "maintain this skill when probed weekly for at least 4 weeks," which will demonstrate that she has both mastered and retained it.

Why does best practice include these elements for annual goals?

These elements ensure that all team members understand and agree on the specific learning or behaviors expected of a student. This is essential for three reasons:

1. Teachers use well-written goals to plan accurate instruction and learning activities for students. Nebulous or nonspecific annual goals are too likely to lead to undirected instruction and wasted learning time.

2. Teachers use these elements to design and administer accurate assessments of student progress toward the annual goals. Continual monitoring guides teachers to make changes in curriculum and instruction if a student is not progressing.

3. Team members refer to the components of well-written annual goals to verify the student's final achievement.

May I see examples of poorly written annual goals?

Certainly. Here are two examples that omit important elements.

Example 1: *Edgar will understand how to write accurately.*

YES (NO) a statement of conditions in which the behavior will be performed

YES (NO) a statement of observable, measurable behavior

YES (NO) a statement of criterion for mastery

YES (NO) a statement of generalization

YES (NO) a statement of maintenance

Example 2: *When asked by the teacher, Katya will behave appropriately for 3 consecutive weeks.*

(YES) NO a statement of conditions in which behavior will be performed

YES (NO) a statement of observable, measurable behavior

YES (NO) a statement of criterion for mastery

YES (NO) a statement of generalization

(YES) NO a statement of maintenance

Now it's your turn.

1. Here is an annual goal for Maddie. Write the phrase from the goal next to the matching element in the list below. Then check your answer with our suggestions in the appendix.

   Annual Goal
   When given a grocery list with five or fewer items and a $10.00 bill, Maddie will select and purchase all the items on the list with fewer than five prompts in three different grocery stores over a 3-week period.

   Conditions: _____

   Behavior: _____

   Criteria: _____

   Generalization: _____

   Maintenance: _____

2. Here is one part of a PLAAPF statement for Suraj, a second-grade boy. Your task is to write an annual goal to address this need, making sure to include all five elements. Check your answer with the suggestions in the appendix.

   PLAAPF Statement
   When directed by the teacher to be seated, Suraj yells defiantly and refuses to sit at his desk 80% of observed instances across settings.

   Annual Goal

   Conditions: _____

   Behavior: _____

   Criteria: _____

   Generalization: _____

   Maintenance: _____

Each IEP team might create annual goals that differ from the goals written by other teams, based on the team's knowledge of the student's preferences and capabilities and the demands of the educational environments in which the student is served. So the goal we suggest in the appendix serves only as an example of what a team might decide is appropriate for Suraj.

Does the IEP team need to include benchmarks or short-term objectives for annual goals?

This requirement varies. Previous versions of IDEA required that all annual goals include benchmarks or short-term objectives. Now the law requires these provisions only for students who take alternate assessments aligned to alternate achievement standards.

What does this mean for the team?

The IEP team must determine a student's need for alternate assessments aligned to alternate achievement standards and then add benchmarks or short-term objectives to the annual goals. Alternate standards and alternate assessment procedures apply only to the small percentage of students whose disabilities inhibit them from progressing comparably to their peers without disabilities in the general curriculum; these students cannot be judged by the same standards.

What are benchmarks and short-term objectives?

Benchmarks and short-term objectives are two ways to break down annual goals into smaller, measurable parts. They enable teachers to monitor student achievement in intervals and report progress to IEP team members more than once per year. The two terms are often used interchangeably, but we see benchmarks and short-term objectives as different ways to describe expected progress.

Benchmarks, which are concerned with a single skill, have three components:

1. They break down one skill into major milestones to be achieved throughout the year.

2. They describe levels of increasing performance for the target skill, such as accuracy, fluency, or difficulty.

3. Many of them include dates by which students are expected to meet the milestones.

For example, traveling from your home to your school requires that you proceed to the first turn, continue to the second turn, and so on, until you drive into the school parking lot. Your goal is to travel from your home to the school, and the turns represent benchmarks that must be met accurately and sequentially.

Short-term objectives describe multiple, related but distinct and nonsequential skills necessary to achieve the annual goal. For example, preparing to travel from your home to your school might require you to dress, fix your hair, and eat breakfast. These tasks are related to preparing to leave, but they need not be completed in a particular sequence.

Would you explain the terms and accompanying processes in more detail?

Certainly. We provide descriptions, examples, and figures to help explain the differences between benchmarks and short-term objectives.

Benchmarks

Benchmarks set out major milestones to achieving an annual goal. These goals can be broken down into benchmarks in a variety of ways, including performance, assistance level, task analysis, generalization, and a combination. Here are some sample phrases from benchmarks showing these four ways to break down annual goals.

Performance. The goal can be benchmarked according to within-child factors like the level of accuracy, fluency, difficulty, or quality required to ensure that the student has acquired the skill or knowledge.

- Sort three types of kitchen utensils at least 67% correctly by October 31 (accuracy)
- Read 50 words correctly per minute by January 31 (fluency)
- Put on shoes; then put on shoes and fasten Velcro; finally, put on shoes, then tie shoe laces by April 30 (difficulty)
- Drill holes in key rack with uniform depth and diameter by May 15 (quality)

Figure 3. Benchmarks *Performance.*

This example shows the "needs to" portion of a present levels of academic achievement and functional performance (PLAAFP) statement, followed by the annual goal divided into benchmarks with projected achievement dates and with three criteria for increased accuracy throughout the school year.

			Annual Goal
		Benchmark 2	Increased accuracy, fluency, difficulty, or quality
	Benchmark 1	Increased accuracy, fluency, difficulty, or quality	Read 2.5-level fiction and nonfiction text with **80%** accuracy by June 1.
PLAAFP "Needs to" Statement	Increased accuracy, fluency, difficulty, or quality	Read 2.5-level fiction and nonfiction text with **60%** accuracy by March 1.	
Student needs to read 2.5-grade-level fiction and nonfiction text with 80% accuracy.	Read 2.5-level fiction and nonfiction text with **40%** accuracy by December 1.		

Assistance level. The goal can be benchmarked according to the level of outside assistance needed to complete the task. An example of this progressive assistance level follows:

- Use computer mouse with *full physical* prompting in 10 weeks.
- Use computer mouse with only *verbal prompting* in 15 weeks.
- Use computer mouse with *no prompting* in 20 weeks.

Figure 4. Benchmarks *Assistance Level.*

This example shows the "needs to" portion of a present levels of academic achievement and functional performance (PLAAFP) statement, followed by the annual goal divided into benchmarks with projected achievement dates showing four ways to provide decreasing levels of assistance throughout the school year.

				Annual Goal
			Benchmark 3	No prompt
		Benchmark 2	Model	Complete dressing tasks with **no prompting** by April 1.
	Benchmark 1	Partial prompt	Complete dressing tasks with **modeling** by February 1.	
PLAAFP "Needs to" Statement	Full prompt	Complete dressing tasks with **partial physical prompting** by December 1.		
Student needs to complete dressing tasks without prompting.	Complete dressing tasks with **full physical prompting** by October 1.			

Task analysis. The goal can be task-analyzed: broken down into components to be mastered sequentially in order to accomplish the complete goal. For example, the goal of counting to 100 could use the following benchmarks:

- Rote count 1 to 10 in 5 weeks.

- Rote count 1 to 20 (requires -teen numbers) in 8 weeks.

- Rote count 1 to 100 (uses the same pattern after 20) in 15 weeks.

Figure 5. Benchmarks *Task Analysis.*

This example shows the "needs to" portion of a present levels of academic achievement and functional performance (PLAAFP) statement, followed by the annual goal divided into benchmarks with projected achievement dates showing four sequential steps necessary to meet the annual goal.

				Annual Goal
			Benchmark 3	Skill 4 **Fold** clothes by May 1.
		Benchmark 2	Skill 3 **Dry** clothes by February 1.	Skill 3 Dry clothes.
	Benchmark 1	Skill 2 **Wash** clothes by December 1.	Skill 2 Wash clothes.	Skill 2 Wash clothes.
PLAAFP "Needs to" Statement	Skill 1 **Sort** clothes by October 1.	Skill 1 Sort clothes.	Skill 1 Sort clothes.	Skill 1 Sort clothes.
Student needs to sort, wash, dry, and fold clothes.				

Generalization. A goal can be benchmarked by increasing the areas of generalization to other cues, materials, people, times of day, or environments. For example, the IEP team may choose to benchmark an IEP goal to care totally for toileting needs with the most salient form(s) of generalization.

- Totally care for toileting needs when reminded by the teacher by October 15. (cue)

- Totally care for toileting needs using a urinal by March 30. (materials)

- Totally care for toileting needs while other students are in the school restroom by November 1. (people)

- Totally care for toileting needs before lunch by February 28. (time of day)

- Totally care for toileting needs using restrooms in the community by April 1. (environment)

Figure 6. Benchmarks *Generalization.*

This example shows the "needs to" portion of a present levels of academic achievement and functional performance (PLAAFP) statement, followed by the annual goal divided into benchmarks with projected achievement dates showing three ways to generalize the skill across the school year. It also shows the annual goal broken down into two, rather than three, benchmarks.

			Annual Goal
		Benchmark 2	3 Different persons, environments, cues, times, and/or materials Purchase food from **street vendor** by May 1.
	Benchmark 1	2 Different persons, environments, cues, times, and/or materials Purchase food in **sit-down restaurant** by February 1.	Purchase food in sit-down restaurant.
PLAAFP "Needs to" Statement	1 Person, environment, cue, time, and/or material Purchase food in **fast-food restaurant** by November 1.	Purchase food in fast-food restaurant.	Purchase food in fast-food restaurant.
Student needs to purchase food in fast-food restaurants, in sit-down restaurants, and from street vendors.			

These criteria are not mutually exclusive. You may decide to combine two or more of them in writing benchmarks for annual goals.

Figure 7. Benchmarks *Combination of Performance and Assistance Level.*

This example shows the "needs to" portion of a present levels of academic achievement and functional performance (PLAAFP) statement. The annual goal is divided into benchmarks with projected achievement dates and with increasing criteria for accuracy combined with levels of decreasing assistance throughout the school year.

				Annual Goal
			Benchmark 3	
		Benchmark 2	Increased accuracy, fluency, difficulty, or quality Follow picture-based directions, **80%** accuracy, **peer modeling,** by April 1.	Increased accuracy, fluency, difficulty, or quality Follow picture-based directions, **80%** accuracy, **no assistance,** by June 1.
	Benchmark 1	Increased accuracy, fluency, difficulty, or quality Follow picture-based directions, **70%** accuracy, **partial physical prompts,** by February 1.		
PLAAFP "Needs to" Statement	Increased accuracy, fluency, difficulty, or quality Follow picture-based directions, **60%** accuracy, **full physical prompts,** by November 1.			
Student needs to follow picture-based directions with at least 80% accuracy without assistance.				

How many benchmarks must the team write?

The law uses the plural terminology "a description of benchmarks or short-term objectives"; thus, there must be at least two benchmarks for each annual goal.

May I see an example of a goal with benchmarks?

Here is an example of benchmarks for Angelica using task analysis.

Annual Goal
When in a social setting with peers, Angelica will initiate conversation and discuss a range of at least five different topics with at least five-word sentences and/or phrases over at least 50% of observed occurrences, and maintain this skill when probed weekly for at least 4 weeks.

Benchmarks

a. When with a new friend or an acquaintance and using a picture prompt, Angelica will initiate conversation in at least 50% of observed occurrences and maintain this skill when probed weekly for at least 4 weeks.

b. When with a new friend or an acquaintance and using a picture prompt, Angelica will discuss a new topic in at least 50% of observed occurrences and maintain this skill when probed weekly for at least 4 weeks, on at least five different topics.

c. When with a new friend or an acquaintance and using a picture prompt, Angelica will discuss a topic using at least five-word sentences and/or phrases in at least 50% of observed occurrences and maintain this skill when probed weekly for at least 4 weeks, on at least five different topics.

Angelica's benchmarks are task-analyzed to occur in sequence and can be illustrated as follows:

Figure 8. Angelica's benchmarks task analyzed.

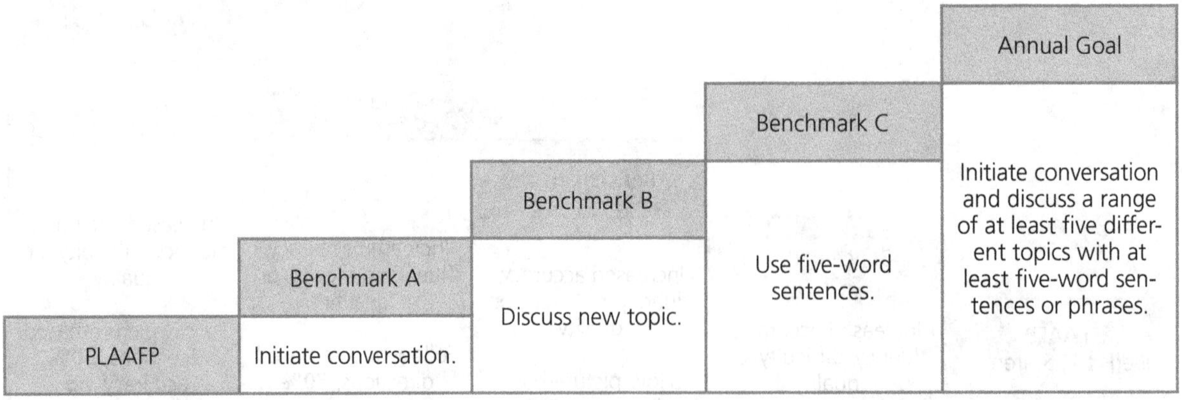

May I see examples of incompletely written benchmarks?

Here are two examples of incompletely written benchmarks:

1. Demetri will cook a frozen meal in a microwave oven without burning it.

YES (NO) a statement of conditions in which the behavior will be performed

(YES) NO a statement of observable, measurable behavior

(YES) NO a statement of criterion for mastery ("without burning it")

YES (NO) a statement of generalization

YES (NO) a statement of maintenance

2. When Olivia's nose is runny and her teacher asks her to wipe it, Olivia will wipe her nose.

(YES) NO a statement of conditions in which the behavior will be performed

(YES) NO a statement of observable, measurable behavior

YES (NO) a statement of criterion for mastery

YES (NO) a statement of generalization

YES (NO) a statement of maintenance

Time to Practice

Write two benchmarks for Benjamin's annual goal, using *each* of the given methods. When you finish, compare your answers with our suggestions in the appendix.

Annual Goal
When presented with 10 items and asked to count them, Benjamin will point to and count the items orally and correctly with no prompts.

Performance
1. Benchmark _____
2. Benchmark _____

Assistance Level
1. Benchmark _____
2. Benchmark _____

Task Analysis
1. Benchmark _____
2. Benchmark _____

Generalization
1. Benchmark _____
2. Benchmark _____

Short-Term Objectives

Short-term objectives describe multiple, nonsequential, distinct, yet related skills necessary to achieve the annual goal. Short-term objectives are determined by listing the individual skills that must be mastered to accomplish the annual goal. Like benchmarks, short-term objectives describe the conditions, the behavior, and the criteria for mastery. They may also include statements for generalization and maintenance.

Figure 9. Short-Term Objectives *Distinct Skills.*

This example shows the "needs to" portion of a present levels of academic achievement and functional performance (PLAAFP) statement. The short-term objectives describe three nonsequential, distinct, yet related skills necessary to meet the annual goal.

PLAAFP "Needs to" Statement	Short-Term Objective 1	Short-Term Objective 2	Short-Term Objective 3	Annual Goal
Student needs to cover mouth when coughing or sneezing, rub lotion on dry skin, and put lip balm on dry lips.	Skill 1 Cover mouth and nose when coughing or sneezing.	Skill 2 Rub lotion on hands and arms.	Skill 3 Apply balm on dry or chapped lips.	Skills 1–3 Cover mouth and nose when coughing or sneezing, rub lotion on hands and arms, apply lip balm on dry or chapped lips.

Let's look at a math example for Spencer.

Annual Goal
When assessed on the state alternate assessment at the end of the school year, Spencer will increase his math skills to a 1.6 grade level in at least 80% of the tested subdomains (EE.2.MD.7; EE.1.OA.1; EE.2.G.1).

Short-Term Objectives
a. When given a clock, Spencer will tell the time to the hour, the half hour, and 15-minute increments (using his communication device or verbally) with at least 80% accuracy, with at least two different types of clocks (digital or analog), and maintain the skill when probed weekly for 2 weeks.

b. When given addition and subtraction problems within 20, Spencer will solve the problems with at least 80% accuracy, under three different conditions, and maintain this skill when probed weekly for 2 weeks.

c. When asked to draw a shape (e.g., triangle, quadrilateral, pentagon, hexagon), Spencer will draw the identified shape with at least 80% accuracy, under three different conditions, and maintain this skill when probed weekly for 2 weeks.

We had better practice this.

Write two short-term objectives for Benjamin's annual goal. When you finish, check your answers with our suggestions in the appendix.

Annual Goal

When presented with 10 items and asked to count them, Benjamin will point to and count the items orally and correctly with no prompts.

1. Short-term objective: _____

_____

2. Short-term objective: _____

_____

Let's summarize the elements of measurable annual goals, benchmarks, and short-term objectives.

1. Measurable annual goals describe the conditions, the behavior, and the criteria for achievement. They may also contain statements of generalization and maintenance.

2. Benchmarks break down annual goals into smaller, measurable parts at designated time intervals.

3. Short-term objectives break down annual goals into nonsequential, distinct skills without reference to specific time intervals.

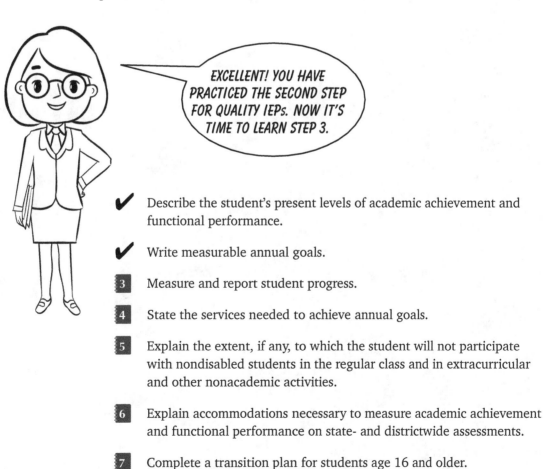

EXCELLENT! YOU HAVE PRACTICED THE SECOND STEP FOR QUALITY IEPs. NOW IT'S TIME TO LEARN STEP 3.

✔ Describe the student's present levels of academic achievement and functional performance.

✔ Write measurable annual goals.

3 Measure and report student progress.

4 State the services needed to achieve annual goals.

5 Explain the extent, if any, to which the student will not participate with nondisabled students in the regular class and in extracurricular and other nonacademic activities.

6 Explain accommodations necessary to measure academic achievement and functional performance on state- and districtwide assessments.

7 Complete a transition plan for students age 16 and older.

References

Yates, J. (2014, April). *Exceeding the standard: A practical guide to developing and implementing IEP goals aligned with the Common Core State Standards*. Paper presented at the Council for Exceptional Children Convention & Expo, Philadelphia, PA.

Measure and Report Student Progress

We have discussed the importance of writing appropriate annual goals in measurable terms so that the team agrees on the specific expectations for student improvement during the year. Why is measurement so important? Consider this parallel: If you make a New Year's resolution to lose 25 pounds by December but do not weigh yourself until October, you may not meet your goal. Regular monitoring of your weight would enable you to watch your progress and determine whether you need to adjust your behavior. Similarly, regular measurement of student learning shows team members whether the student is making adequate progress. If progress is not measured, the team cannot track the success of instruction, and the teacher cannot make necessary changes to help the student meet annual goals.

Parents are part of the individualized education program (IEP) team, but they are not in school to observe their child's daily progress. Therefore, the Individuals with Disabilities Education Improvement Act (IDEA) requires the team to include the following in the IEP:

- A description of **how** the student's progress toward meeting the annual goals will be measured.

- A commitment to **when** periodic reports of the student's progress toward meeting the annual goals will be provided to the parents.

Let's examine each of these requirements.

How do I describe how progress will be measured?

You describe how progress will be measured by noting how data will be collected for each annual goal. You may begin by looking at the behavior and the criterion described in the goal and determining how that behavior can best be measured (e.g., percentage correct, number correct, rate, frequency, latency, or duration).

For example, Ricky's second behavior goal states, "When in the cafeteria, Ricky will take his place in line and remain there without pushing or otherwise removing other students for 100% of opportunities **as measured by** observer tallies three times in one week." This means that the special education teacher, school psychologist, behavior specialist, or other trained observer will be in the cafeteria to tally the number of times Ricky gets in line and the number of times he either pushes or does not push other students. These tallies can then be converted to a percentage to determine progress toward the goal. When Ricky meets 100% compliance three times in one week, he has achieved the goal.

You probably recall that well-written annual goals address involvement and progress in the general curriculum and include criteria for achievement. The same types of assessment data used to create present levels of academic achievement and functional performance (PLAAFP) statements can be used to measure progress on goals. In Step 1, we described two general data sources:

1. Formal assessment (e.g., *Key Math*, *Kaufman Test of Educational Achievement*, *Vineland Adaptive Behavior Scales*)

2. Informal assessment (e.g., criterion-referenced tests, curriculum-based measures, work samples, student self-monitoring records, skills checklists, behavior checklists, home skills checklists)

The IEP must include the assessment used to measure progress, such as the name of a formal test, designation of a student work sample, plan for a teacher observation, or checklist for behavior.

Let's see how this applies to IEPs for Jameelah, Spencer, and Ricky.

Jameelah's Annual Goal

Given stories, dramas, and poems of eighth-grade complexity read aloud to her and weekly opportunities to practice, Jameelah will say or write answers to literal and inferential questions about theme, characters, and events with at least 90% accuracy on two samples of each text type, as measured by teacher observation records and informal written work (CCSS.ELA-LITERACY.RI.8.10).

Measurement Method
The target behavior is to "say or write answers to literal and inferential questions about theme, characters, and events with at least 90% accuracy on two samples of each text type." The measurement methods are teacher observation records and work samples.

- Spoken answers can be recorded by the teacher on an **observation checklist**.

- Written answers can be recorded by Jameelah or a peer to be graded by the teacher.

Rationale
The IEP team chose a teacher observation records and a work sample because Jameelah will answer questions directly from assigned readings. Because the goal states that Jameelah will "say or write," either a teacher checklist or written work will be a direct record of Jameelah's responses.

Spencer's Benchmark

When Spencer needs to fasten his clothes (e.g., after using the restroom, when putting on his coat), he will correctly fasten his clothes within 1 minute with no prompts, four out of five times weekly with at least three different fasteners (e.g., snaps, zippers, buttons), and maintain this skill when probed weekly for 2 consecutive weeks.

Measurement Method
The measurement method is a task analysis checklist completed by the teacher during each skill probe.

Rationale

The team chose a **checklist** as a simple method for tracking Spencer's accomplishment of each step in fastening his clothes. The checklist, with the date included, allows the teacher to determine when Spencer has met the criterion and maintained the skill.

Ricky's Annual Goal for Behavior

When requested or directed by the teacher, Ricky will comply without removing materials for at least 90% of opportunities in any class period over 5 days, as measured by student self-monitoring and teacher observation records.

Measurement Method

The measurement methods are student self-monitoring and teacher observation records. To verify the percentage of opportunities during which Ricky complies with the teacher's request or direction without removing materials, the special educator will teach him to monitor and record his behavior after each incident. The teacher will also record requests or directives, along with Ricky's responses, on a simple tally sheet.

Rationale

The IEP team chose these informal **behavior checklist** methods for two reasons. First, self-monitoring is a proven strategy that can help Ricky learn to check and modify his own behavior, especially if the self-monitoring is paired with a reinforcement system. Second, the tally system provides the teacher with quick frequency data about Ricky's percentage of compliance that can be used later to check Ricky's accuracy at self-monitoring. The team needs the data but wisely avoids burdening the classroom teacher with a complex and time-consuming measurement system (always a good idea for preserving good relations with colleagues!).

Time to Practice

Read Miakiah's and Alonzo's goals (below) and write the following about each:

1. An appropriate measurement method

2. Your rationale for choosing the method

Then check your answers with ours in the appendix.

Mikiah's Annual Goal

When presented with 20 items of clothing, Mikiah will sort the clothing to prepare for laundering, with at least 80% accuracy, once weekly for three consecutive weeks.

Measurement Method

☐ formal assessment   ☐ criterion-referenced tests   ☐ curriculum-based assessments

☐ checklists   ☐ work samples   ☐ self-monitoring

Rationale

Why this method?: _____

Alonzo's Annual Goal

When given a worksheet with 10 items of each type and when directed by the teacher, Alonzo will add and subtract single-digit items and write answers with no errors.

Measurement Method

☐ formal assessment   ☐ criterion-referenced tests   ☐ curriculum-based assessments

☐ checklists   ☐ work samples   ☐ self-monitoring

Rationale

Why this method?: _____

_____

How do I decide and how do I indicate when periodic reports of progress toward annual goals will be provided?

You must provide regular reports to parents regarding their children's progress, thus updating parents more often than the yearly IEP meetings. IDEA requires that reports of IEP goal progress be issued at least as often as school report cards. Schools and districts use a variety of reporting methods, and you should check with your supervisors to determine the preferred method in your school.

An IEP form might include a section for indicating when the reporting will be provided, such as the one shown here:

	Weekly	Biweekly	Monthly	Quarterly	Semiannually
Home note	X				
Progress report					
Parent conference					X
Report card				X	
Other					

How does this step in the IEP process affect classroom practice?

Assessing and reporting each student's progress affects classroom practice by requiring the teacher to do three things: measure, monitor, and report.

- *Measuring* is the act of administering some type of assessment to describe a student's academic or social behavior.

- *Monitoring* is the act of comparing student achievement to desired goals.

- *Reporting* provides oral or written information regarding student achievement.

Measuring

A teacher measures progress frequently to determine whether the students are progressing at the rate necessary to achieve their goals. Measures are more frequently informal than formal, and the measurement schedule depends on the type of learning or behavior being assessed. The teacher may measure student progress several times a day, once a day, several times a week, once a week, or at some other appropriate interval.

Monitoring

A teacher monitors student progress by comparing measurement data with appropriate benchmarks. Schoolwide student progress is usually compared to state or district standards, grade-level or class progress is often monitored by comparison to other students, and individual progress is compared to individual goals. Comparison with individual goals is the practice for students with IEPs. To determine if a student is making adequate progress toward IEP goals, a teacher must monitor frequently enough to either verify adequate progress or make necessary instructional changes to increase achievement.

Reporting

Teachers or other service providers use monitoring data to report students' progress to parents at least as often as reports for students without disabilities.

Let's summarize how to measure and report student progress toward annual goals.

The IEP must do the following:

1. Describe **how** the student's progress toward meeting the annual goals will be measured.

2. Describe **when** periodic reports of the progress the student is making toward meeting the annual goals will be provided.

WELL DONE! YOU HAVE STUDIED AND PRACTICED STEP 3. NOW WE WILL MOVE TO STEP 4.

✔ Describe the student's present levels of academic achievement and functional performance.

✔ Write measurable annual goals.

✔ Measure and report student progress.

4 State the services needed to achieve annual goals.

5 Explain the extent, if any, to which the student will not participate with nondisabled students in the regular class and in extracurricular and other nonacademic activities.

6 Explain accommodations necessary to measure academic achievement and functional performance on state- and districtwide assessments.

7 Complete a transition plan for students age 16 and older.

4 *State the Services Needed to Achieve Annual Goals*

The statement of special education and related services on the individualized education program (IEP) describes how and where specialized instruction will be provided to help students achieve their annual goals. You will remember that present levels of academic achievement and functional performance (PLAAFP) statements describe what the student is achieving at the time of the IEP, and the annual goals describe what the student should achieve in one year.

YOU CAN THINK OF SPECIAL EDUCATION AND RELATED SERVICES AS THE BRIDGE BETWEEN ACHIEVEMENT RIGHT NOW AND ACHIEVEMENT IN A YEAR'S TIME.

The IEP team begins by reviewing the student's current achievements, as noted in the PLAAFP statements, and considering the student's annual goals in order to determine which services will be required to meet them. This review is an important evaluative process enabling team members to make collaborative decisions for the student's education based on empirical evidence. Once services have been determined, the team decides how the services will be provided.

Unfortunately, some teams make these decisions in the wrong order. They decide where the student should be served and what services will be provided—then they write the annual goals and PLAAFP statements. Quality IEPs that are legally correct are developed with the student's goals driving services and placement.

Special education and related services accomplish two purposes: (1) They help the student achieve annual goals, and (2) they do this in the *least restrictive environment*. Our discussion of special education and related services requires you to understand the least restrictive environment, so we define this term now.

What is the least restrictive environment?

The Individuals with Disabilities Education Improvement Act (IDEA) requires that students with disabilities be educated in the least restrictive environment (LRE), which means that these students are educated with their peers without disabilities to the maximum extent appropriate, as determined by the IEP team. *Restrictive* in this case means any situation in which students with disabilities are educated in special classes or separate schools, or have otherwise been removed from the general class. Removing a student from the general classroom is appropriate when the IEP team determines that the nature or severity of the student's disability prevents satisfactory learning, even with supplementary aids or services provided.

What alternative placements are possible for students with disabilities?

If the IEP team determines that a student's needs cannot be met in the regular classroom, then the team members look at the continuum of alternative placements that are more likely to meet the student's needs. This continuum moves from least to most restrictive and usually includes the following:

* Full inclusion in regular classes

* Less than half of each day in a resource classroom

* More than half of each day in a resource classroom

* Instruction in a self-contained classroom within the school

* Instruction in a separate school

* Instruction in the child's home

* Instruction in a hospital or institution

Are there other considerations when determining appropriate placement?

Yes. IDEA requires IEP teams to ensure that the student's placement is

* determined at least annually,

* based on the student's IEP, and

* as close as possible to the student's home.

This means that the student is educated in the school he or she would attend if he or she did not have a disability unless another selection is made with which the parent agrees. Some districts cluster students with severe disabilities in specialized classrooms in certain schools, which might cause a student to be served in a school other than the one closest to home.

In addition, when selecting the LRE, the team must consider any potential harmful effects on the child or on the quality of services needed. The student should not be removed from an age-appropriate regular class solely because of needed modifications in the general education curriculum. When the student's needs can be met in the regular class by modifying the curriculum or providing supplemental aids or services, the student should not be removed to a more restrictive environment.

BECAUSE THE LRE IS DETERMINED BY EACH IEP TEAM, THE LRE FOR ONE STUDENT MAY BE DIFFERENT FROM THAT FOR ANOTHER STUDENT WITH THE SAME DISABILITY.

What services are described on the IEP?

The law requires that the IEP state the services to be provided *to the student* or *on behalf of the student* and also specify the program modifications or supports provided for *school personnel* to help the student. IDEA requires that services be based on peer-reviewed research to the extent practicable. Thus, strategies, methods, and materials used to provide specially designed instruction should be well grounded in empirical research that substantiates effectiveness. You can understand how important this requirement is if you have noticed the cycle of unproven instructional fads and trendy practices that come and go in education.

Services provided to or on behalf of the student include

- special education services,

- related services, and

- supplementary aids and services.

Services provided for school personnel include

- program modifications and

- supports for teachers.

All of the provided services must help the student

- advance appropriately toward attaining the annual goals,

- engage and make progress in the general education curriculum,

- participate in extracurricular and other nonacademic activities, and

- participate with peers both with and without disabilities in academic learning and additional activities.

Let's look at the services for students and school personnel.

What are special education services?

Special education services refer to *specially designed instruction* to meet the unique needs of students with disabilities, as described in their annual goals. Specially designed instruction includes teaching, learning, practice, and assessment strategies that help students achieve annual goals; this may involve adaptations to the general curriculum.

Who receives special education services?

Students whose annual IEP goals require specially designed instruction receive special education services. They are eligible for services only if they have been classified with a disability and have a current IEP. IDEA states that children with disabilities are those ages 3 to 9 who experience developmental delays or those up to age 22 who are classified with one of these 12 disabilities:

- Autism

- Deaf-blindness

- Hearing impairment, including deafness

- Intellectual disabilities

- Multiple disabilities

- Orthopedic impairment

- Other health impairment

- Serious emotional disturbance

- Specific learning disabilities

- Speech or language impairment

- Traumatic brain injury

- Visual impairment, including blindness

Your state may use different terms for some disability classifications, so be sure to learn your local terminology.

Who provides special education services?

Special education services are provided by or under the direction of licensed special educators. Special education para-educators may also provide services to students with disabilities, but they must do so under the direction of a licensed special educator.

Where are special education services provided?

Special education services are provided across a continuum of educational placements, including the regular class, a separate special education class, a separate special education facility, the child's home, or a hospital or other institution. A student in any educational placement can receive special education services. The services provided and the places where they are delivered are determined by the IEP team within the requirements for LRE.

IT IS IMPORTANT TO UNDERSTAND THAT SPECIAL EDUCATION REFERS TO SERVICES, **NOT** TO A CERTAIN PLACE IN A BUILDING.

How do I write special education services on the IEP?

Here is an example of special education services for Ricky.

Special Education Services to Achieve Annual Goals and Advance in General Curriculum

Service	Location	Time	Frequency	Begin Date	Duration
Reading fluency and comprehension	Regular Class **Special Class** Other:	*45 min*	**Daily** Weekly Monthly	*9/16*	**1 year** Other:

The IEP team has decided that the special education teacher will need to provide specially designed reading instruction for Ricky and that it will occur in a special class (the resource room).

What are related services?

Related services refer to transportation, as well as developmental, corrective, and other supportive services needed to help a student with disabilities benefit from special education. The following services are included:

- Counseling, including rehabilitation counseling

- Early identification and assessment of disabling conditions

- Interpreting services

- Medical services

- Orientation and mobility services

- Physical and occupational therapy

- Psychological services

- Recreation, including therapeutic recreation

- School nurse services

- Social work services

- Speech-language pathology and audiology services

- Transportation

Who receives related services?

Any student with an IEP may receive related services that are necessary for the student to benefit from special education. For example, a student may receive specialized instruction for specific learning disabilities and also receive speech-language services. Another student may require orientation and mobility services but not receive any other specially designed instruction.

Who provides related services?

Each related service is provided by or under the direction of the professional who is licensed to provide it. IEP teams commonly include a school psychologist, a speech-language pathologist, a physical therapist, or an occupational therapist, depending on each student's unique needs.

Where are related services provided?

Related services can be provided in a regular classroom, a separate room or office, or an extracurricular setting, depending on student needs.

How do I write related services on the IEP?

Here are the related services added to Ricky's IEP.

Related Services to Benefit from Special Education

Service	Location	Time	Frequency	Begin Date	Duration
Behavior intervention	Regular Class Special Class **Other:** **School psychology office**	20 min	**Daily** **Weekly** 2x Monthly	9/16	**1 year** Other:

Notice that Ricky's IEP specifies school psychology services to address his goals to improve behavior. The school psychologist will teach Ricky replacement behaviors to eliminate his outbursts and refusal to work, and the teacher will then reinforce desired behaviors in her classroom. However, this level of detail is not required on the IEP; the team only needs to note that Ricky will receive behavior intervention provided by the school psychologist.

What are supplementary aids and services?

Supplementary aids and services refers to aids, services, and other supports provided in regular education classes or other education-related settings to enable students with disabilities to be educated with nondisabled students to the maximum extent appropriate (notice the emphasis on LRE). These services are provided when the IEP team determines that the student will need adjustments or modifications to the general curriculum or additional instruction in order to meet IEP goals.

When supplementary aids and services are needed, the IEP team may determine that teachers must make adjustments or modifications in one or more of the following areas:

1. The ways teachers present information

   - A student with visual impairments may need large-print materials.

   - A student who is deaf and lip-reads may need to see the teacher's face when he is speaking.

   - A student who cannot process sequential instructions may need the teacher to model each of the steps and provide a step-by-step list to follow.

2. The ways students complete tasks

   - A student who has poor motor skills may need to dictate written expression to a scribe.

   - A student who has difficulty grasping math concepts may need instruction with manipulative objects to learn new skills or concepts.

   - A student may require assistive technology for speaking, listening, reading, or writing.

3. The ways teachers assess student learning

   - A student who processes information slowly may need additional time to complete a test.

   - A student who attends school only in the afternoon due to a health impairment will need tests scheduled for afternoons.

   - A student who is highly distractible may need to be tested in a distraction-free environment.

   - A student who has a visual impairment or reading difficulty may need to have a test dictated.

   - A student who cannot speak may need to point to indicate answers to test items.

4. The ways teachers structure the environment

   - A student who is easily distracted may need reduced-distraction seating or work areas, away from windows, fish tanks, open doors, or other areas with heavy traffic or sensory stimuli.

   - A student using a walker will need wide enough pathways to access all areas of the classroom.

   - A student who uses a wheelchair will need materials and equipment placed within reach.

   - A student with visual impairments will need a stable, predictable physical environment in which change is rare in order to navigate easily in the classroom.

   - A student who has a hearing impairment will need visual access to any information that other students learn by hearing, such as the public address system or movies and videos shown in class.

   - A student who has difficulty learning and following classroom routines may benefit from a posted daily schedule to anticipate transitions between activities.

Who receives supplementary aids and services?

Any student with an IEP may receive supplementary aids and services if the services are necessary for the student to benefit from special education. For example, a student who cannot use a regular computer keyboard may need an adapted keyboard with larger keys. Another student may require large-print materials but may not require specially designed instruction.

Who provides supplementary aids and services?

Supplementary aids and services may be provided by a regular class teacher, para-educator, special educator, related service provider, or other qualified school personnel. The school administrator may authorize a supplementary aid if it requires the purchase of equipment or alterations to the school facilities.

Where are supplementary aids and services provided?

Supplementary aids and services are provided in the regular class or in other curricular or extra-curricular environments to meet the student's IEP goals. The primary focus of providing supplementary aids and services is to facilitate student success in the regular class and in other environments with nondisabled peers.

How do I write supplementary aids and services on the IEP?

Let's look at an example. Here is the supplementary aids and services statement from Spencer's IEP.

Program Modifications and/or Supplementary Aids and Services in Regular Classes

Supplementary Aids and Services	Frequency
Personal communication device	*Daily* Weekly Monthly

Spencer uses a personal communication device to communicate most of his needs, so the team notes this supplementary aid on his IEP.

What are program modifications or supports?

Program modifications or supports assist teachers in meeting the unique and specific needs of students with disabilities. Let's briefly explore these terms.

- *Program modifications* include interventions and accommodations necessary for the teacher to help the student achieve IEP goals. For example, a student whose behavior interferes with learning will need a program of positive behavioral supports to learn more appropriate and productive behaviors. The IEP team would discuss these needs, describe the necessary modifications on the IEP, and provide the support the teacher needs to implement the program.

- *Supports* include special training for teachers to help them meet unique or specific needs of students in the classroom. For example, a teacher may need to be taught how to enter new vocabulary words into a student's communication device so the student can use the vocabulary as other students are assigned to do.

Who receives program modifications or supports?

School personnel who are responsible for addressing a student's goals receive program modifications or supports, which are noted on the IEP.

Who provides program modifications or supports?

School personnel may receive program modifications or supports from a special educator, a para-educator, a related service provider, a staff developer, or another education professional.

Where are program modifications or supports provided?

Program modifications or supports can be provided in the regular classroom or in other curricular or extracurricular environments to meet the student's IEP goals. These modifications and supports should help the student achieve annual goals in the least restrictive environment.

How do I write program modifications or supports on the IEP?

Spencer's IEP includes the following program support for his teachers.

Program Modifications and/or Supplementary Aids and Services in Regular Classes

Modifications/Personnel Support	Frequency
Autism training; positive behavior support training and consultation	Daily Weekly **Monthly**

Spencer's regular class teacher has never taught a child with autism, so the team has determined that a specialist in autism, augmentative communication, and behavioral issues will provide training and consultation to this teacher and to Spencer's special educator.

What special factors does the team consider?

Depending on the needs of the student, the IEP team must consider what IDEA calls *special factors*, as noted in the following:

- If the student's behavior interferes with his or her learning or the learning of others, the IEP team will consider positive behavior interventions and supports to address the problems.

- If the student has limited proficiency in English, the IEP team will consider the student's language needs as they relate to his or her IEP.

- If the student is blind or visually impaired, the IEP team must provide for using and instructing in Braille, unless they determine after an appropriate evaluation that the student does not need this instruction.

- If the student is deaf or hard of hearing or has other language or communication needs, the IEP team must consider those needs, including enabling the student to communicate directly with classmates and school staff members in her or his usual method of communication (e.g., sign language).

- The IEP team must consider the student's need for assistive technology devices or services.

Here is an example from Spencer's IEP that shows how special factors can be indicated on an IEP. It indicates that he needs positive behavior instruction and support, communication and language services, and assistive technology.

Applicable Special Factors

Factor	Not Needed	In IEP
Positive behavior instruction and support when behavior impedes learning of student or others		✓
Language needs for student with limited English proficiency	✓	
Braille instruction for student who is blind or visually impaired	✓	
Communication and/or language services for student who is deaf, is hard of hearing, or has other communication needs		✓
Assistive technology devices or services		✓

How does the team decide what services the student needs?

The team considers the student's PLAAFP statements and annual goals, and then decides the types of service that will best help the student achieve the goals. For example, if you look at Angelica's IEP, you can see that she has annual goals in math, language arts, social/emotional skills, communication, functional life skills, and career/vocational. You will also note that the IEP team determined that a range of services for Angelica are necessary to achieve the goals.

May I see examples of IEP team decisions for determining services?

Sure. Refer to the IEPs for the four students who have served as examples throughout the instructions in Step 4. You will see the services listed after the annual goals. This IEP format is a good reminder that IEP teams first establish annual goals and then decide which services are needed to meet those goals.

Time to Practice

Refer to Spencer's IEP and answer the following questions. Then compare your answers with the appendix.

1. What special education services does Spencer require?

2. What related services does Spencer require?

3. What supplementary aids and services in the regular classroom does Spencer require?

4. What program modifications and supports do Spencer's teachers require?

5. What special factors did the IEP team choose?

6. Explain why you think the IEP team recommended these services.

What decisions does the IEP team make regarding the date, frequency, location, and duration of services to be provided?

Once the team decides which special education and related services are required, they record this information on the IEP and then specify the following:

- **Date.** The IEP should designate when the special education and related services will begin. The IEP is in effect when it is signed by the team, but services might not begin until the next school day.

- **Frequency.** The IEP should also indicate how often the services will be provided. The decision about frequency of services is made by the IEP team and agreed on by those who provide the services.

CHECK WITH YOUR SCHOOL OR DISTRICT TO FIND OUT WHETHER TIME INCREMENTS ARE TO BE RECORDED IN MINUTES OR HOURS, AND BY THE DAY, WEEK, OR MONTH.

- **Location.** Location for the services should also be included. Remember, the team is required by IDEA to provide services in the least restrictive environment.

- **Duration.** The team must also decide on and record the length of time the services will be provided. IDEA requires the team to review the IEP at least annually, but the team may review and/or rewrite the IEP more often if needed to meet the individual needs of the student.

These important aspects of the IEP provide specific information to parents, teachers, and students regarding the number and type of services the student will receive, and when and where those services will be provided. The IEP form or program will have a place to specify this information, perhaps similar to the examples above.

Is there anything tricky to watch for at this stage of IEP development?

Yes, there is. A common error occurs when the team confuses the term *service* with the term *location*. For example, it is incorrect for the team to write "special class" as a service; "special class" is a *location*. The type of service would be specially designed instruction, speech therapy, life skills instruction, or some other such designation.

May I see some examples of this part of IEP decision making?

Sure. Just look back at the examples provided above.

Are there special considerations for providing services to secondary students with IEPs?

Yes. IDEA requires that IEP teams address transition planning for students age 16 and older. You will learn this important process in Step 7.

Let's summarize the requirements for Step 4.

1. Determine which services will be provided *to* or *on behalf of* the student. These services may include

    - special education services,
    - related services, and
    - supplementary aids and services.

2. Determine which services will be provided for *school personnel.* These services may include

    - program modifications and
    - supports.

3. Make sure that all of the provided services will help the student

    - advance appropriately toward attaining the annual goals,
    - engage and make progress in the general education curriculum,
    - participate in extracurricular and other nonacademic activities, and
    - participate with peers both with and without disabilities in academic learning and additional activities.

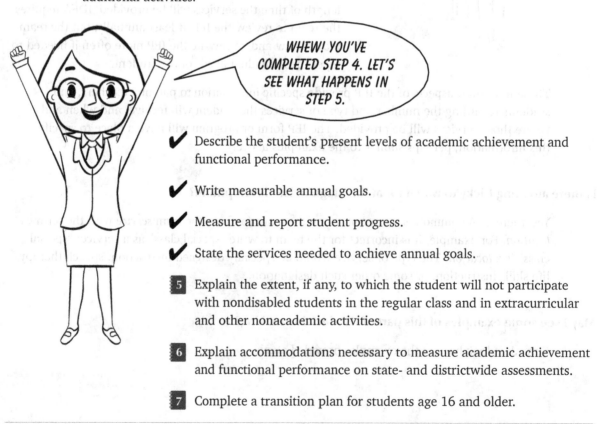

WHEW! YOU'VE COMPLETED STEP 4. LET'S SEE WHAT HAPPENS IN STEP 5.

✔ Describe the student's present levels of academic achievement and functional performance.

✔ Write measurable annual goals.

✔ Measure and report student progress.

✔ State the services needed to achieve annual goals.

5 Explain the extent, if any, to which the student will not participate with nondisabled students in the regular class and in extracurricular and other nonacademic activities.

6 Explain accommodations necessary to measure academic achievement and functional performance on state- and districtwide assessments.

7 Complete a transition plan for students age 16 and older.

Explain the Extent, if Any, to Which the Student Will Not Participate with Nondisabled Students in the Regular Class and in Extracurricular and Other Nonacademic Activities

The law, through the least restrictive environment (LRE) requirement, assumes that every student with disabilities will be involved and progress in the general education curriculum. All students with disabilities will also participate with nondisabled students in regular classes, as well as in extracurricular and other nonacademic activities. When a student is not to participate as just described, the individualized education program (IEP) team must determine why such participation is not appropriate and include a statement of the extent to which the student will not participate.

What are the concerns about excluding students with disabilities from regular classes and activities?

Concerns about excluding students from any aspect of the regular school program are related to the area of exclusion. When students do not participate in regular classroom activities, they do not benefit from teachers' content knowledge and from opportunities to learn with and from their peers without disabilities. And when students are restricted from extracurricular or other nonacademic activities, they miss important social interactions and opportunities to enrich their life experiences in the same ways as do students without disabilities.

REMEMBER, THE SPIRIT AND INTENT OF LRE IS TO ENSURE THAT ALL STUDENTS HAVE ACCESS TO THE GENERAL CURRICULUM TO THE MAXIMUM EXTENT APPROPRIATE.

What is meant by the terms *regular class,* **extracurricular activities,** and *other nonacademic activities?*

These terms should not be confused with the general curriculum. The general curriculum can be taught in a separate special education setting, but students would be excluded from participating with their nondisabled peers. The following examples will help you understand what is meant by these terms.

The Regular Class

Typically the regular class is where students with disabilities receive instruction in the general curriculum with nondisabled peers. This is the designation for grade-level classes in elementary schools and for required or elective classes in secondary settings.

Extracurricular Activities

Extracurricular activities are supplementary to the general curriculum and are not required by state curriculum standards. They generally vary from school to school and may include activities such as the following:

- Different types of sports
- Peer leadership
- Game-type activities such as Knowledge Bowl
- Different types of school clubs

Nonacademic Activities

Nonacademic activities are part of the school day, but they are not directly related to mandated curriculum or extracurricular activities. Such activities may include:

- Breakfast
- Lunch
- Recess
- School assemblies
- Class parties

How does the IEP team determine if a student will not participate in regular classes and activities?

The IEP team must make this determination by deciding whether the nature or severity of the disability would preclude participation in regular classes and activities even with the use of supplementary aids and services. For example, Martha has a medical condition that is exacerbated when she comes into contact with other people who have contagious diseases. Knowing that her fragile health condition adversely affects her ability to learn alongside her peers, her team decided to exempt her from participating in activities in which she is in close contact with other students.

IEP teams must be cautious to avoid excluding a student from a regular school program based solely on the disability classification. Most students who receive special education services can participate in the regular school program with varying degrees of adaptation or accommodation.

How does the team address this decision on the IEP?

The IEP must include an explanation of the extent to which the student will not participate in the regular school program. You will need to learn what your district or state requires for this part of the IEP. The following example, from Spencer's IEP, is a statement of nonparticipation and is included under Participation in Regular Class, Extracurricular, and Nonacademic Activities:

Participation in Regular Class, Extracurricular, and Nonacademic Activities

The student will participate in the regular class and in extracurricular and other nonacademic activities except as noted in special education and related services or listed here:

> *Spencer will not participate in lunch in the cafeteria at the same time as other students or in in-school assemblies. Due to his need to have intensive, individualized instruction in a quiet environment, he will not participate in some regular class instruction.*

Spencer's present levels of academic achievement and functional performance (PLAAFP) statement shows his extreme sensitivity to noise and to crowds of people. The IEP team's decision to exempt him from noisy and crowded school activities, including cafeteria lunch and school assemblies, is stated clearly on the IEP. Remember the requirement for a free and *appropriate* public education in the least restrictive environment? Spencer's IEP team decided that, because of the effects of his disability, these two school activities are not appropriate for him; fortunately, this decision does not significantly restrict his education environment.

Your Turn!

Read each of the following vignettes and write your advice for the IEP team regarding nonparticipation. When you are finished, compare your recommendations with those in the appendix.

1. Boston was born with cerebral palsy, which limits his fine and gross motor movement.

   The student will participate in the regular class and in extracurricular and other nonacademic activities except as noted in special education and related services or as listed here:

   _____

   _____

2. Asher receives specially designed behavior supports in all regular classes.

   The student will participate in the regular class and in extracurricular and other nonacademic activities except as noted in special education and related services or as listed here:

   _____

   _____

Let's summarize the extent of nonparticipation in the regular class and in extracurricular and other nonacademic activities.

1. Students with disabilities are expected to participate in regular classes and activities.

2. The three areas in which students with disabilities participate are
   - the regular class,
   - extracurricular activities, and
   - other nonacademic activities.

3. The IEP must include a statement explaining the extent to which a student will not participate in the regular class and/or in extracurricular and other nonacademic activities.

4. This statement can list specific classes or activities in which the student will not participate.

WELL DONE! YOU HAVE PRACTICED THE FIFTH STEP FOR WRITING QUALITY IEPs. IT'S TIME TO LEARN STEP 6.

✔ Describe the student's present levels of academic achievement and functional performance.

✔ Write measurable annual goals.

✔ Measure and report student progress.

✔ State the services needed to achieve annual goals.

✔ Explain the extent, if any, to which the student will not participate with nondisabled students in the regular class and in extracurricular and other nonacademic activities.

6 Explain accommodations necessary to measure academic achievement and functional performance on state- and districtwide assessments.

7 Complete a transition plan for students age 16 and older.

6 Explain Accommodations Necessary to Measure Academic Achievement and Functional Performance on State- and Districtwide Assessments

Consistent with the goal of involvement and progress in the general education curriculum, students with disabilities are to participate with nondisabled students in state- and districtwide assessments. Their participation ensures that education professionals are accountable for the appropriate progress of all students. The law requires the individualized education program (IEP) team to include a statement of any individual accommodations that are necessary to measure a child's academic achievement and functional performance on state- and districtwide assessments. If the team determines that a student with disabilities cannot reasonably participate in all or part of one of these assessments, even with accommodations, then the team must select an alternate assessment for that student.

How might students with disabilities participate in state- or districtwide assessments?

Students with disabilities can participate in state- or districtwide assessments under any of several conditions, based on the IEP team's decision. Not all states offer all assessment options, so you need to check your state regulations to learn which options are available. The following choices are generally offered:

- Regular assessment of grade-level academic content standards based on grade-level academic achievement standards.

- Regular assessment of grade-level academic content standards with appropriate *accommodations* based on grade-level academic achievement standards.

- Alternate assessment of grade-level academic content standards based on grade-level academic achievement standards.

- As explained in Step 1, alternate assessment of grade-level academic content standards based on *alternate* academic achievement standards.

When are students with disabilities assessed on state- and districtwide assessments?

Students with disabilities are tested on the same schedule as those without disabilities. Federal law requires systematic assessment of student progress in specified grades for certain subjects (e.g., language arts, math, and science); however, your school district might require additional tests. Be sure to check with your school or district regarding the scheduling of state- and district-wide assessments.

THE NO CHILD LEFT BEHIND (NCLB) ACT REQUIRES ALL STUDENTS, INCLUDING THOSE WITH DISABILITIES, TO PARTICIPATE IN STATE- AND DISTRICTWIDE ASSESSMENTS.

What is regular assessment of grade-level academic content standards based on grade-level academic achievement standards?

This means students with disabilities take the same tests under the same conditions as students without disabilities.

How does the team decide that a student will participate in this option?

The IEP team may decide that a student with a disability who has performed at capacity on previous assessments will take the same tests under the same conditions as students without disabilities. This decision must be made with substantial evidence that taking the tests under standardized conditions does not prevent the student from demonstrating competency.

What is regular assessment of grade-level academic content standards with appropriate *accommodations* based on grade-level academic achievement standards?

This means that students with disabilities take the same tests as students without disabilities but under different conditions. The IEP team must remember that participating with accommodations means that there are no changes to test content or administration that *fundamentally alter or lower the standard or expectations of the assessment.*

How does the IEP team decide that a student will participate in this option?

The team should consider whether the student requires accommodations for classroom instruction and tests. If accommodations are required in the course of daily learning and classroom assessments, then the student will most likely require the same or similar accommodations for state- and districtwide assessments, depending on the content being assessed.

How does the IEP team select appropriate accommodations for state- and districtwide assessments?

The team can select appropriate accommodations based on answers to these or similar questions:

- What accommodations does the student regularly use in the classroom and on tests of content similar to that covered on the state- or districtwide assessments?

- What is the student's perception of the efficacy of the accommodations regularly used? Has the student been willing to use the accommodations?

- What evidence is available from parents, teachers, or others about the efficacy of an accommodation?

- Have there been difficulties administering the selected accommodations? (National Center for Learning Disabilities, 2005)

While the difficulty of providing specific accommodations should not warrant dismissing them, IEP teams may select different accommodations that are equally effective but not as intrusive or difficult to administer.

What are some examples of assessment accommodations?

As we look at examples, please remember that accommodations do not fundamentally change the content or administration of the test in ways that alter or lower the standard or expectations of the assessment. Be sure to check your state or district guidelines to learn which accommodations are acceptable within this definition. Here are several examples of accommodations for various domains of test administration.

Setting

- Provide a distraction-free environment such as a study carrel.

- Provide special furniture, such as an adjustable-height desk for a wheelchair.

- Provide a small-group setting.

Scheduling

- Provide extended testing time within the same day.

- Administer the test in several sessions within total time allowance.

Test Format

- Provide a Braille edition.

- Present the test in the student's native language.

- Increase spacing, including fewer items per page or only one sentence per line.

- Provide magnification or amplification equipment.

Test Directions

- Read directions to the student.

- Provide recorded directions.

- Simplify language in order to clarify or explain.

- Repeat directions for subtasks.

Test Procedures

- Read content aloud, except for reading subtests in which specific skills being assessed preclude reading aloud.

- Use sign language for orally presented test items.

- Provide written copies of orally presented materials that are found only in the administrator's manual.

Student Response Format

- Allow an adult to enter the student's answer on a computer-based test.

- Permit the student to answer by pointing, signing, typing, responding orally, or providing another nonwritten response.

- Audio-record the student's responses.

- Provide a template or placeholder for the answer document.

May I see an example of selected accommodations on an IEP?

Sure. Refer to Jameelah's IEP, and notice that her present levels of academic achievement and functional performance (PLAAFP) statement indicates that she does not read well on material above the fifth-grade level. Under the section Participation in State and District Assessment, the team noted that Jameelah should have the *test directions* read aloud in English for language arts, math, and science, and that the math and science *test items* should be read aloud in English. The language arts test items would not be read aloud because doing so would fundamentally alter or lower the standard or expectations of the reading assessment.

Practice choosing appropriate accommodations for students.

Read each of the following cases and write your suggestions for appropriate accommodations for state- and districtwide assessments. You can refer to the examples provided above. Then compare your answers with our suggestions in the appendix.

---

1. Amara has fine motor limitations that prevent her from holding or using a pencil.

   Suggested accommodation: _____

   _____

2. Derrick has visual impairments that prevent him from reading print of normal size.

   Suggested accommodation: _____

   _____

3. Kalappan's attention deficit disorder significantly impairs his ability to concentrate in groups larger than three or four students.

   Suggested accommodation: _____

   _____

What is alternate assessment of grade-level academic content standards based on grade-level academic achievement standards?

This option addresses the same content and holds students to the same expectations as does the regular grade-level test, but students participate in some way other than the usual paper-and-pencil or computer-based test. For example, students may demonstrate content mastery through work samples aligned with the grade-level standards.

IEP TEAMS MUST BE CAUTIOUS IN SELECTING THE ALTERNATE MEANS BY WHICH STUDENTS WILL DEMONSTRATE THEIR SKILLS BECAUSE THESE ALTERNATE TESTS MUST BE COMPARABLE TO THE REGULAR ASSESSMENTS, AND THEY MUST BE VALID AND RELIABLE IN ORDER TO BE ELIGIBLE FOR DETERMINING THE STUDENTS' ANNUAL PROGRESS.

How does the team decide that a student will participate in a particular option?

Similar to determining appropriate accommodations, the team considers ways that the student successfully demonstrates learning in the classroom on comparable content. If sufficient evidence shows that the student demonstrates achievement or ability more accurately in an alternate way, then the IEP team may choose this option.

What is alternate assessment of grade-level academic content standards based on *alternate* academic achievement standards?

This option means students are tested on grade-level content but with altered expectations for performance. As the term indicates, modifications *modify* (alter) some aspect of the way the test is presented or the way the student responds to test items.

How does the team decide that a student will participate with this option?

As with accommodations, the team considers any modifications required for the student to be successful in daily learning. The student will most likely require the same or similar modifications for state- and districtwide assessments.

How does the team select appropriate modifications for state- and districtwide assessments?

As with accommodations, the team considers the modifications needed for the student to experience academic success in the classroom: whether the student prefers and uses these modifications, if the modifications have been effective, and whether other modifications might be less difficult to administer while obtaining similar results.

May I see some examples of assessment modifications?

Certainly. Here are several examples of modifications for some domains of test administration.

Test Format

- Highlight key words or phrases.

- Place visual cues on the test form, such as arrows or "Stop" signs.

- Assist students by pointing.

- Reduce the number of test items.

Test Procedures

- Audio-record or read the entire test when it includes reading subtests.

- Sign or cue the test.

- Read aloud complex multiple-step math questions one step at a time.

- Allow a calculator to be used for noncalculator tests or subtests.

- Allow use of manipulative math objects that are not provided to all students.

Student Response Format

- Allow reference materials not provided to all students (e.g., a multiplication table).

- Allow use of a spell and/or grammar check for tests or subtests of spelling or composition.

- Provide a scribe for tests or subtests of writing.

Remember that modifications cause the content or administration of the test to be fundamentally changed in ways that alter or lower the standard or expectations of the assessment. If the test publisher does not allow certain changes to the test content or administration, those changes would be considered modifications.

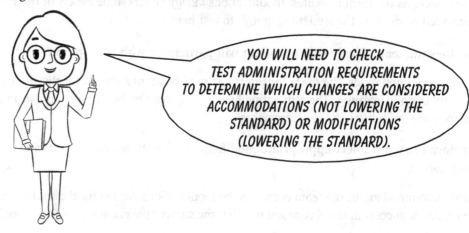

YOU WILL NEED TO CHECK TEST ADMINISTRATION REQUIREMENTS TO DETERMINE WHICH CHANGES ARE CONSIDERED ACCOMMODATIONS (NOT LOWERING THE STANDARD) OR MODIFICATIONS (LOWERING THE STANDARD).

Let's practice choosing appropriate modifications.

Read each of the following cases and write your suggestions for appropriate modifications for state- and districtwide assessments. Compare your answers with our suggestions in the appendix.

---

1. Duong's visual impairment prevents him from reading print on a reading test, but he has good listening comprehension skills.

   Suggested modification: _____

   _____

2. Novia has a health impairment that significantly reduces the amount of time she can work without resting.

   Suggested modification: _____

   _____

What is alternate assessment aligned with grade-level academic content standards scored against alternate academic achievement standards?

As described in Step 1, this alternate assessment is based on alternate achievement standards that are linked to grade-level content standards but have been reduced in complexity, depth, or breadth. These tests reflect an alternate level of expectations compared to regular assessments or alternate assessments based on grade-level achievement standards. In general, alternate achievement standards must

- be aligned with a state's academic content standard,

- promote access to the general curriculum, and

- reflect professional judgment of the highest achievement standards possible.

STEP 1 EXPLAINS THAT THE NO CHILD LEFT BEHIND ACT RESTRICTS THIS TESTING TO NO MORE THAN 2% OF STUDENTS IN A STATE OR DISTRICT.

How does the team decide that a student will participate in this option?

The team decides by considering established guidelines for having a student participate in this type of testing rather than in the standard state- or districtwide assessment. This option applies to students who

- have the most significant cognitive disabilities and do not reach grade-level academic standards, even with appropriate instruction, and/or

- participate in a curriculum more closely aligned with an alternate curriculum rather than the general curriculum.

What must be included on the IEP if a student takes an alternate assessment?

IEP teams are given authority to administer alternate assessments appropriate for measuring students' academic achievement and functional performance. However, the types of assessments from which these teams can choose depend on individual state or district regulations. The types of assessments generally available include checklists, portfolios, and task performance demonstrations, including the use of assistive technology. These assessments must have an explicit structure as well as clearly delineated scoring criteria and procedures. They should also be valid, reliable, accessible, objective, and consistent with nationally recognized professional and technical standards.

The IEP must include a statement explaining why

- the student cannot participate in the regular assessment, and

- the particular alternate assessment selected is appropriate for the student.

What alternate assessments can the team select?

Ms. Mentor answers that question for you.

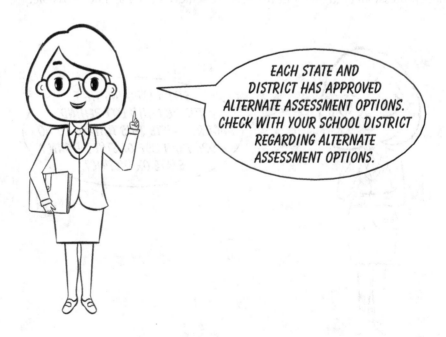

EACH STATE AND DISTRICT HAS APPROVED ALTERNATE ASSESSMENT OPTIONS. CHECK WITH YOUR SCHOOL DISTRICT REGARDING ALTERNATE ASSESSMENT OPTIONS.

May I see an example of this kind of statement?

Of course. Look at Spencer's IEP and you will see the following statements:

Alternate Assessment

State why student cannot participate in regular assessment.

Spencer's skills in math and language arts are approximately 1 to 2 years behind his nondisabled peers; his poor communication skills, limited attention span, and inability to write impair his ability to demonstrate his achievement successfully on standardized tests.

State why selected alternate assessment is appropriate.

Spencer was administered the state alternate assessment at the beginning of this year and was able to demonstrate his skills, given multiple testing breaks, prompts to stay on task, concrete examples, and multiple explanations of the tasks, in a one-on-one setting.

Let's practice choosing appropriate alternate assessments.

Read each of the following cases and mark your suggestions for either standard assessment or alternate assessment. Compare your answers with ours in the appendix.

---

1. Ezzie requires substantial adaptations and supports to access the grade-level content meaningfully, requires intensive individualized instruction to acquire and generalize knowledge, and is unable to demonstrate achievement of academic content standards on a paper-and-pencil test, even with accommodations.

   ☐ Standard assessment   ☐ Alternate assessment

2. Aisha's significant cognitive disability and orthopedic impairments prevent her from participating successfully in standardized assessments, even with accommodations and modifications.

   ☐ Standard assessment   ☐ Alternate assessment

Let's summarize how the team explains necessary accommodations for state- and districtwide assessments.

The team considers the student's strengths, needs, and abilities, and then chooses one of these options, as allowed by the particular state and/or district, and plans accordingly:

- Regular assessment of grade-level academic content standards based on grade-level academic achievement standards.

- Regular assessment of grade-level academic content standards with appropriate *accommodations* based on grade-level academic achievement standards.

- Alternate assessment of grade-level academic content standards based on grade-level academic achievement standards.

- Alternate assessment of grade-level academic content standards based on *alternate* academic achievement standards.

ONE MORE STEP TO CONSIDER. THE IEP TEAM MUST COMPLETE A **TRANSITION PLAN** FOR STUDENTS AGE 16 AND OLDER, WHICH IS THE SUBJECT OF STEP 7.

✔ Describe the student's present levels of academic achievement and functional performance.

✔ Write measurable annual goals.

✔ Measure and report student progress.

✔ State the services needed to achieve annual goals.

✔ Explain the extent, if any, to which the student will not participate with nondisabled students in the regular class and in extracurricular and other nonacademic activities.

✔ Explain accommodations necessary to measure academic achievement and functional performance on state- and districtwide assessments.

7 Complete a transition plan for students age 16 and older.

Reference

National Center for Learning Disabilities. (2005). *No Child Left Behind: Determining appropriate assessment accommodations for students with disabilities.* New York, NY: Author. Retrieved from http://www.ldonline.org/article/10938

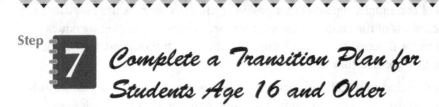

Complete a Transition Plan for Students Age 16 and Older

Transition planning is a student-centered process of structuring course work and other educational experiences to prepare the student for transition from school to adult life. Transition planning results in a formal document that is individualized to the needs and aspirations of the student for adult living.

The individualized education program (IEP) team must develop a transition plan beginning with the IEP in effect when the student turns 16, or younger if determined appropriate by the IEP team. This plan must be reviewed and updated annually until the student no longer receives special education services.

Does transition planning ever apply to students younger than 16?

Yes. The IEP team may begin transition planning and services at an earlier age if the effects of the student's disability are such that more time is required to prepare for transition to adult life.

What are the requirements for a transition plan?

The transition plan must include these components:

- Appropriate, measurable postsecondary goals based on age-appropriate transition assessments related to
  — Education
  — Training
  — Employment
  — Independent living skills, where appropriate

- Transition services, including courses of study, necessary to assist the student in reaching the goals

- A statement that the student has been informed of transfer of adult rights no later than one year before the student reaches the age of majority

How does the team accomplish transition planning?

Let's answer this question by explaining how the team addresses each of the three elements.

1. *Measurable postsecondary goals*
   The first step in transition planning is for the student, in conjunction with the IEP team, to explore aspirations for the student's future. The law requires the goals to be based on data from appropriate transition assessments. This is best accomplished when the IEP team

and representatives of community agencies that provide transition services use assessment results to guide discussions of the student's career interests, desires for continuing education, and expectations for independent adult living. The student's interests are then translated into postsecondary goals in four areas:

- **Education.** Goals for education include what the student wants to study in a postsecondary setting, where the student wants to study, admission requirements for the desired school and program, and associated financial obligations. Goals related to courses necessary for graduation can also be written.

- **Training.** Training refers to specific skills necessary for desired employment, such as word processing, equipment operation, food handling, interpersonal relations, or carpentry.

- **Employment.** Goals for employment focus on the student's desired trade or occupation. The target occupation may be available to the student immediately upon high school graduation or may require specific training or education.

- **Independent living.** Goals in this area relate to the type of housing the student desires upon completion of school as well as transportation necessary to access community services and activities.

2. *Transition services, including courses of study, necessary to assist the student in reaching the goals*

The second step in transition planning is to determine what services must be provided during the school years to help the student reach the postsecondary goals. Because transition services may be provided outside the school, the team must invite a representative of any participating agency that will be responsible for providing or paying for transition services. Such agencies may include public or private job training services, welfare services, mental health agencies, or other community-based programs. Transition services may include any or all of the following:

- **Instruction,** including courses of study that address academic or skill-training preparation for achieving postsecondary goals.

- **Related services** necessary for the student to achieve annual IEP goals.

- **Community experiences** provided outside the school, such as community-based job exploration, job-site training, banking, shopping, transportation, health care, counseling, and recreation activities.

- If appropriate, the acquisition of **daily living skills**, such as grooming, laundry care, food preparation, and budgeting.

- If appropriate, the provision of a **functional vocational evaluation** to determine the student's readiness for employment. This evaluation involves a comprehensive assessment of the student's vocational preferences and skills to work in both general and specific work settings. The evaluation can be accomplished with formal or informal assessments of the student's strengths, aptitudes, interests, work experiences, and other relevant attributes.

3. *A statement that the student has been informed of the transfer of adult rights no later than one year before the student reaches the age of majority*
The third requirement for transition planning is to inform the student of the pending transfer of adult rights, if any, to the student at the age of legal adult status in the state of residence. This requirement must be completed no later than one year *before* the student reaches the age of majority. Check with your local school or district to see if a special form is used for this process.

Summary of Performance

The Individuals with Disabilities Education Improvement Act (IDEA) requires schools to summarize the academic achievement and functional performance of students with disabilities who graduate or who no longer receive special education after age 22. The school must provide a copy of the summary to the student. This summary of performance should provide enough information so that the individual can meet disability qualification standards for the Americans with Disabilities Act and other laws pertinent to adults with disabilities.

May I see an example of a transition plan?

Most assuredly. Look at Angelica's transition plan appended to her IEP. You will find each requirement addressed on the form.

NOTE THAT THE IEP AND THE TRANSITION PLAN ARE COMPLEMENTARY DOCUMENTS. IEP TEAMS SERVE SECONDARY STUDENTS MOST EFFECTIVELY WHEN IEP GOALS ARE ADDRESSED WITH EDUCATIONAL SERVICES AS WELL AS COMMUNITY-BASED SERVICES; HOWEVER, THE PRIMARY RESPONSIBILITY RESTS WITH THE EDUCATIONAL AGENCY.

Your Turn

Select the service(s) your IEP team would recommend for Josh, a 17-year-old adolescent with orthopedic impairments, in order to meet the annual goal listed below. Check your answers with our suggestions in the appendix.

Annual Goal

When Josh arrives at work from the city bus, he will independently wheel himself into the building, clock in, and begin his work, with no verbal prompts, for at least 4 weeks.

Services:

☐ Education

☐ Training

☐ Employment

☐ Independent living

☐ Daily living skills

CONGRATULATIONS! YOU HAVE LEARNED AND PRACTICED ALL SEVEN STEPS FOR WRITING HIGH-QUALITY IEPs. NOW YOU SHOULD BE READY TO SERVE ON A TEAM OF PARENTS AND PROFESSIONALS WHO ARE COMMITTED TO SERVING ALL STUDENTS WITH DISABILITIES IN AN ETHICAL AND PROFESSIONAL MANNER. WITH SOME PRACTICAL EXPERIENCE, YOU WILL BECOME COMFORTABLE WRITING HIGH-QUALITY IEPs.

Appendix

ANSWERS TO EXERCISES

STEP 1

Example of Present Levels of Academic Achievement and Functional Performance (PLAAFP) for Samuel

Samuel can do one-digit addition and subtraction without renaming, but he cannot add or subtract multiple digits without renaming and cannot multiply and divide. He can dictate simple sentences when given a subject, but he cannot compose and write simple sentences when given a subject. He can identify his backpack, but he cannot place school materials in the backpack when directed. He can use the restroom independently, but he cannot fasten his pants or wash his hands before leaving the restroom. He can follow two-step requests in order, but he does not wait his turn in line; he can talk with his friends but interrupts others in their conversations. To progress in the general curriculum, Samuel needs to use place-value understanding and properties of operations to perform multi-digit arithmetic (CCSS. MATH.CONTENT.4.NBT.B). And with guidance and support from peers and adults, he should also develop and strengthen writing as needed by planning, revising, and editing (CCSS.ELA-LITERACY.W.4.5). He also needs to improve self-help and socialization skills.

Error in Kingston's PLAAFP

This PLAAFP entry provides a "can do" statement but no "cannot" or "does not do" statement. A more specific statement would include additional information related to this skill; for example, "Kingston initiates and sustains conversations with peers and can call his friends on the telephone. He does not ask his teacher for assistance when needed. He does not distinguish between appropriate and inappropriate comments to female peers."

Error in Evangeline's PLAAFP

This statement provides information unrelated to Evangeline's disability, which is in reading, not penmanship. A better statement would include specific information about her reading skills; for example, "Evangeline has mastered kindergarten reading standards. She cannot decode words or read fluently at grade level."

Error in McCoy's PLAAFP

McCoy's statement provides a vague description of his social/behavioral skills. A more descriptive PLAAFP would include specific information about his social/behavioral skills, such as "When directed to engage in work-related tasks, McCoy throws his school materials and yells at the teacher an average of eight times per day. He complains daily that he does not like school. McCoy's behavior interferes with his progress in the general academic and social curriculum."

Annual Goal for Maddie

Conditions: When given a grocery list with five or fewer items and a $10.00 bill

Behavior: Maddie will select and purchase all the items on the list

Criteria: with fewer than five prompts

Generalization: in three different grocery stores

Maintenance: over a 3-week period

Annual Goal for Suraj

Conditions: When directed by the teacher to be seated

Behavior: Suraj will sit quietly at his desk

Criteria: within 5 seconds, in 90% of instances,

Generalization: in each of his classes

Maintenance: over a 4-week period

Benjamin's Benchmarks

When presented with 10 items and asked to count them, Benjamin will point to and count the items orally and correctly with no prompts.

Performance

1. *Benchmark:* In 10 weeks, when presented with 10 items and asked to count them, Benjamin will point to and orally count the items with at least 50% accuracy.

2. *Benchmark:* In 20 weeks, when presented with 10 items and asked to count them, Benjamin will point to and orally count the items with at least 80% accuracy.

Assistance Level

1. *Benchmark:* In 10 weeks, when presented with 10 items and asked to count them, Benjamin will point to and orally count the items correctly with verbal prompts, with 10 out of 10 correct.

2. *Benchmark:* In 20 weeks, when presented with 10 items and asked to count them, Benjamin will point to and orally count the items correctly with no prompts, with 10 out of 10 correct.

Task Analysis

1. *Benchmark:* In 10 weeks, when presented with five items and asked to count them, Benjamin will point to and orally count the items correctly with no prompts, with five out of five correct.

2. *Benchmark:* In 20 weeks, when presented with 10 items and asked to count them, Benjamin will point to and orally count the items correctly with no prompts, with 10 out of 10 correct.

Generalization

1. *Benchmark:* In 10 weeks, when presented with 10 identical items and asked to count them, Benjamin will point to and orally count the items correctly with no prompts, with 10 out of 10 correct.

2. *Benchmark:* In 20 weeks, when presented with 10 dissimilar items and asked to count them, Benjamin will point to and orally count the items correctly with no prompts, with 10 out of 10 correct.

Benjamin's Short-Term Objectives

1. *Short-term objective:* When presented with 10 items and asked to point to each, Benjamin will point to each item, with 10 out of 10 correct, in three out of three consecutive trials.

2. *Short-term objective:* When presented with 10 items and asked to point to and orally count them, Benjamin will point to and orally count all items, with 10 out of 10 correct, in three out of three consecutive trials.

STEP 3

Measuring Mikiah's Goal
Measurement Method

- ☐ formal assessment
- ☐ curriculum-based assessments
- ☐ work samples
- ☐ criterion-referenced tests
- ☒ checklists
- ☐ self-monitoring

Rationale

An informal teacher checklist will allow the teacher to track progress as the student demonstrates mastery of each component of the skill.

Measuring Alonzo's Goal
Measurement Method

- ☐ formal assessment
- ☒ curriculum-based assessments
- ☐ work samples
- ☐ criterion-referenced tests
- ☐ checklists
- ☐ self-monitoring

Rationale

The criteria require Alonzo to write answers, so an informal curriculum-based measure with 10 items for each operation is most appropriate.

STEP 4

Services for Spencer

1. What special education services does Spencer require?

   - *Specially designed instruction in both regular and special class settings*

2. What related services does Spencer require?

  • *Speech-language services*

3. What supplementary aids and services in the regular classroom does Spencer require?

  • *Personal communication device*

4. What program modifications and supports do Spencer's teachers require?

  • *Autism training; positive behavior support training and consultation*

5. What special factors did the IEP team choose?

  • *Positive behavior instruction, communication and/or language services, assistive technology device*

6. Explain why you think the IEP team recommended these services.

  • *Each of these aids and services are required for Spencer to achieve his IEP goals.*

STEP 5

Boston's Statement of Nonparticipation

The student will participate in the regular class and in extracurricular and nonacademic activities except as noted in special education and related services or as listed here: *Boston will receive physical therapy and adaptive physical education during regular physical education time.*

Asher's Statement of Nonparticipation

The student will participate in the regular class and in extracurricular and nonacademic activities except as noted in special education and related services or as listed here: *Not applicable*

STEP 6

Amara's Accommodation

Dictate answers to scribe.

Derrick's Accommodation

Provide large-print materials or provide magnification equipment.

Kalappan's Accommodation

Take test in study carrel or take test in room with three or fewer students.

Duong's Modification

Teacher reads aloud reading subtests, and student answers comprehension questions orally.

Novia's Modification

Provide more breaks than allowed by test publisher, or reduce the number of test items.

Ezzie's Suggested Assessment

Alternate assessment

Aisha's Suggested Assessment

Alternate assessment

STEP 7

Josh's Transition IEP Goal Services

☐ Education   *This is a job-related goal, and postsecondary education is not mentioned.*

☒ Training   *Josh may need training to achieve this goal.*

☒ Employment   *Josh needs a job in order to achieve this goal.*

☒ Independent living   *Josh needs transportation to get to his work site.*

☐ Daily living skills   *This a job-related goal; daily living skills are not mentioned.*